Education in Business and Industry

THE LIBRARY OF EDUCATION

A Project of The Center for Applied Research in Education, Inc.

G. R. Gottschalk, Director

Categories of Coverage

I	II	III
Curriculum and Teaching	Administration, Organization, and Finance	Psychology for Educators

IV	V	VI
History, Philosophy, and Social Foundations	Professional Skills	Educational Institutions

Education in Business and Industry

CHARLES R. DeCARLO

ORMSBEE W. ROBINSON

The Center for Applied Research in Education, Inc.
New York

LIBRARY OF CONGRESS
CATALOG CARD NO.: 65–28253

PRINTED IN THE UNITED STATES OF AMERICA

Foreword

Our age has been called the atomic age, the air age, the space age, the age of automation. Many characteristics typify our day and age. Yet it is not inconceivable that future historians may look back on this period as the first age in which massive amounts of money were spent to educate people after they started to work.

Education in Business and Industry should be read by everyone who wants to understand the world of today and the world of tomorrow. The meaning of this volume goes far beyond its title. An outstanding characteristic is its description of actual processes and problems of today. Yet it may well contain more of the future than any other book written in the past generation.

About seventy-five years ago business began to spend some money on research. By 1900 the amount might have been as much as $10,000,000; by 1920, $100,000,000; by 1940, $1,000,000,000; by 1965, $12 to $15,000,000,000. These expenditures on research brought about rapid changes and have forced business into massive educational programs. The total research and development in education and training programs of business already is in the $15 to $20,000,000,000 bracket.

So far the expenditures have been most heavily concentrated in large scale manufacturing industries. Similar expenditures are bound to spread to other parts of the business and occupational world. Even now expenditures on research in agriculture which were as small as $200,000,000 a year are forcing farmers to continue their education throughout their working lives. Research expenditures on health which were as small as $1 to $2,000,000,000 are forcing the medical profession to be deeply concerned about constantly continuing the education of doctors and others in the profession.

A national economy that started applying research in a major way to a few areas such as large scale manufacturing, some parts of agriculture, some health areas as well as science areas is now spending another 8 to 12 per cent on the discovery of new knowledge and its use in other areas of the working occupations. Expenditures of this kind will expand to ever widening parts of our economic and social lives. Already research and educational expenditures for the working ages are larger than those for young people and, doubtless, expenditures of this kind for the working population will expand at an even greater rate throughout the rest of the century.

The authors have been actively engaged in educating people after they started work and have had successful results meeting the many problems involved. Their premise that business and industry can survive and prosper only by maintaining continuous educational programs means drastic changes lie ahead for business and industry. It also means education of the young must be changed.

No longer can schools teach the young student all he needs to know. Rather, high schools and colleges must equip the student with the tools to go on learning and with the understanding that study will be a continuous process extending throughout his working life.

For the school administrator, teacher or citizen who must know how these powerful forces are shaping the second half of the twentieth century, here is the book to read.

HAROLD F. CLARK
Professor of Economics
Trinity University
San Antonio, Texas

Education in Business and Industry

Charles R. DeCarlo
Ormsbee W. Robinson

Charles R. DeCarlo and Ormsbee W. Robinson have written a fine volume on a most significant type of education—that which takes place in business and industry. They point out that business and industry are full-fledged partners with public and private lower schools as well as with higher education in meeting the present day American citizens' educational demands. The volume traces the history of this type of education from the guilds to the present day. It points out resemblances with the past and at the same time highlights new developments and trends in business and industry.

DeCarlo and Robinson present the case for education in business and industry basing the structure of their material upon the nature and needs of the modern corporation on the one hand, and of the individual on the other. The programs involved transcend training for specific jobs. They become extensions of general education and, in a manner of speaking, become in-service education for citizenship. Corporations have developed extensive programs for the preparations of managers in order to meet the demand for skilled leadership.

The men who have written this book so skillfully have had extensive graduate education as well as much experience in both higher education and industry.

This monograph fits very well into the Library of Education, completing a cluster of adult education volumes. Former volumes, *University Extension* by Shannon and Schoenfeld and *Adult Education* by Verner and Booth, have treated different elements of education for adult living. Thus, the three enable us to broaden our scope of knowledge in this area.

DANIEL E. GRIFFITHS
Content Editor

Contents

CHAPTER I

A Perspective

Introduction

As America moves into the second half of the twentieth century, the role of education in business and industry assumes a new—and crucial—importance. This is a period characterized by so rapid a rate of growth in all areas of society that the much-used term, *explosion,* is not often misapplied. The "explosion" of population, the "explosion" of technical knowledge—these are elements not only integral in the world of today but also decisive in shaping the world of tomorrow.

The problem, simply put, is one of preparing ever-growing numbers of workers for jobs which are constantly increasing in complexity. The responsibility for the solution of this problem rests not only with the schools but with business and industry as well. Constant advances in technology and the consequent changes in work procedures have altered the very nature of the work process and, with it, the nature of the worker's contribution. These changes have made mandatory a general reorganization of the program of education for participation in the economic process.

The discussion which follows deals with the responsibility of business and industry in the education and training of the labor force, and with the measures adopted or planned to meet this challenge. We will begin by exploring the history of education in business, tracing its development from the apprenticeship system of the Middle Ages to the large-scale and complex corporate training programs of the present. We will compare the educational philosophy and practices in business and industry with those which have evolved in the schools and universities. And, most important, we will describe the business environment within which the programs of training and education are pursued, examining in some detail the forces—technological change, automation, and manpower development needs—which give shape and directions to these educational efforts.

We will be concerned, not only with the general nature of the

educational endeavor in business, but also with the problems and
objectives which attend the particular types of program—whether
it be one designed to provide an individual worker with specific
technological skills or one designed to develop in a group of promising candidates those management and executive skills which have
as their primary aim the efficient operation of the organizational
complex. The discussion will concentrate on those programs found
in the large corporations, but the same realities of economics and
technology which have brought about the organization of these
programs assure their eventual introduction into the smaller companies as well. Another possible development in this regard might
be corporate training centers on an area or regional basis.

Finally, after having examined the background and dimensions
of the problem, and some of the measures taken to solve it, we will
analyze the current issues in education in business and industry,
and the patterns of possible future trends.

History of Education in Business

Apprenticeship.   Probably the oldest form of education in business is the apprenticeship system. This system involves a contract
under the terms of which one person (the master) undertakes to
teach, and another person (the apprentice) undertakes to learn,
some trade or profession. There is evidence in the Code of Ham-
murabi (2285–42 B.C.) that the practice was so firmly established
in ancient Babylonia as to warrant state supervision. References to
the apprenticeship system also appear in Egyptian papyri of the
early Christian era, and in the works of Plato, Aristotle, and Xeno-
phon.

But the apprenticeship system achieved its greatest popularity
and influence during the Middle Ages, when it formed an integral
part of the network of trade guilds and corporations. These guilds
and corporations were composed of skilled workers in various fields.
No one who was not a member of a particular guild was allowed to
practice or to teach that craft or profession. A young man who
wished to learn a given craft apprenticed himself to a master (a
member of the guild governing that particular craft). The term of
apprenticeship varied, but seven years were usually considered the
minimum time within which an individual might learn his craft or
trade and repay his master, by his services, for the training re-

ceived.[1] After an apprentice had given proof of his proficiency in his chosen field, he became himself a master and a member of the guild or corporation, with the right to practice his art and to teach it to others.

The apprenticeship system began to decline during the Elizabethan period when the growth of commerce, the tremendously increased demand for larger and larger quantities of goods, and the emergence of the domestic system of manufacture made close supervision of the training period difficult and unprofitable. But it was the Industrial Revolution that hastened the decline of the traditional form of apprenticeship. The skills required of the workers in the new factories were few and easily learned. Even more important, the process of mechanization, although in its infancy, had already begun: it was no longer feasible to spend seven years learning a particular skill when an improvement of the machinery involved might render the skill obsolete long before the end of that period.

The success of the apprenticeship program is indicated by the fact that in the United States now there are apprentices in training in approximately 300 skilled occupations under ninety trade classifications—bricklaying, glazing, plumbing, tile-setting, painting, paperhanging, photoengraving, and many others. Although their number, in relation to the total number of industrial employees, is probably declining, apprentices do constitute a significant group of skilled production workers, especially in the factory industries, the building trades, and the custom and repair trades.[2]

On the whole, however, the training of the craftsman or laborer in the present-day United States is, for the most part, accomplished through methods other than apprenticeship—among these newer methods are on-the-job-training, formal group instruction, and programmed instruction.

Beyond apprenticeship programs, vocational education, undertaken in the public school system or post-high school private institutes, is being increasingly recognized as one of the prime methods of preparing for entrance to the work force. At this time there is considerable discussion in educational circles, both professional and business, concerning the proper content and purpose of specialized pre-employment training. As we shall see, with the changing nature

---

[1] In England, the Statute of Artificers (1562) made the seven-year period mandatory for anyone who would practice any "trade or mystery."

[2] See also Paul Bergevin, *Industrial Apprenticeship* (New York: McGraw-Hill Book Company, Inc., 1947).

of work to less dependence upon eye-hand coordination and more upon generalized learning skills, the nature of vocational education will loom larger in importance.

Vocational education. In his chapter on "Education and Industry," Professor Cremin[3] traces the development of vocational education in America. He points out that one of the most basic and far-reaching changes in the philosophy and direction of education in the United States was set in motion at the Philadelphia Centennial Exposition in 1876. One of the major themes of the Centennial was the relation of education to national progress, and one of its outstanding attractions was the Russian exhibit, which illustrated a new approach to technical education.

The exhibit was built largely upon the work of Victor Della Vos, Director of the Moscow Imperial Technical School. Della Vos had made a major contribution to Russian education: He had organized *instruction shops* (separate from, and preliminary to, *construction shops*), in which industrial skills were taught by demonstrating mechanical concepts with models and drawings.

The exhibit, and the theories upon which it was based, gave rise to one of the most heated controversies in American education. Then, as now, there were sharp differences of opinion over the value of general education as opposed to technical or vocational education. Emerson White, who had served as president of the National Education Association, "thought it ridiculous for public schools to devote their energies to handicraft training at a time when the machine was assuming an ever greater burden of production."[4] Another opponent of vocational education was William T. Harris, Superintendent of the St. Louis, Missouri, public school system, who warned of the limitations inherent in specialized manual and technical training: "Education that educates the child in the art of self-education is that which the aggregate experience of mankind has chosen for the school."[5]

Labor and management found themselves ranged along opposite sides in the controversy over vocational education. Labor organizations were opposed to manual training because they viewed it as an infringement upon their traditional control over the standards for entrance and membership. Management, on the other hand, found

---

[3] Lawrence A. Cremin, *The Transformation of the School* (New York: Alfred A. Knopf, 1961), p. 35.
[4] *Ibid.*
[5] Cremin, *op. cit.*, p. 31.

that its economic burden might be considerably lightened if the responsibility—and the expense—of training new members of the labor force were to be shifted to the schools.

Despite strong opposition, however, the assumption of responsibility for vocational training by the public school system proved to be inevitable. Neither the young labor organizations nor the established business leaders had shown themselves capable of introducing and maintaining efficient programs. The growing use and increasing complexity of machines in the productive process, the tapering off of the waves of skilled immigrants, and the onset of the decline of agriculture (which brought masses of untrained farm workers to the cities) made it essential that some method be devised to provide skilled workers for the nation's economy.

But even after vocational education had become a standard offering of the public school system, the graduates of these programs proved too few to meet the ever-increasing demands of industry. The gap widened with the striking expansion of the national economy in the latter part of the nineteenth century. As firms began to distribute their goods on a regional and nationwide basis, the demand for skilled workers in every field began to spread to areas far from the central urban locations. There developed a need for accountants who understood the procedures followed by a particular business, technicians who were familiar with the processes involved in a specialized type of engineering, and salesmen who were capable of applying the arts of persuasion to a given market.

By the end of the nineteenth century, the problem had assumed the dimensions of a crisis. Faced with their own pressing need for skilled labor and with the fact that vocational education programs were still too few and too recently instituted, manufacturers found themselves obliged to take on the task of providing their own educational programs for prospective members of the labor force. Their assumption of this responsibility gave rise to the corporation schools.

> At least five such schools were established between 1872 and 1901, and from that time on their numbers increased rapidly. By 1916, it is estimated that some 60,000 boys were attending such schools, and the National Association of Corporation Schools, organized in 1913, is reported to have had 150 members when it merged with the American Management Association in 1922.[6]

---

[6] Harold F. Clark and Harold S. Sloan, *Classrooms in the Factories* (New York: New York University Press, 1958), p. 6.

No rigid pattern governed the development and operation of these corporation schools: each school was planned in accordance with the needs and policies of the particular organization. Some programs provided for the full-time instruction of new workers—not only in technical skills but also in many "classroom" subjects. Others were designed to alternate instruction with actual work experience.

> A few companies made it possible for any employee to attend classes in outside institutions while carrying on part-time work with the company. These were classes in advertising, selling and distributing, business education, English for foreigners, and in more specialized areas applicable to a particular product. One appraisal, comparing the corporation schools with the regular public schools, found the former superior in responsiveness of students, recitation technique, and mental discipline; the latter superior in teaching, breadth of view, and general cultural development. In large measure, however, the corporation schools attained their objectives.[7]

Whether or not the corporation schools suffered by comparison with the public schools in certain respects, there is no doubt that they fulfilled the purposes for which they had been established and —even more important—marked the beginning of a significant phase of business and vocational education. These schools are the precursors of the present-day educational programs instituted by business firms and corporations for the development of individual skills. Their primary aim—the improvement of the quality of people directly involved in the productive process—underlies another important area of business education: the management movement.

The management movement. The management movement, the notion of supervision as a professional activity, may be traced back to the early years of scientific management and the work of Frederick Winslow Taylor, prior to World War I. A knowledge of his theory—that scientific methods could be advantageously applied to business—continues to be essential for an understanding of management concepts and practices. In essence:

> Scientific management is not any efficiency device . . . It is not a new system . . . it is not a bonus system . . . it is not time study; it is not motion study . . . .
> . . . scientific management involves a complete mental revolution on the part of the working man engaged in any particular establish-

---

[7] *Ibid.*

ment of industry—a complete mental revolution on the part of these men as to their duties toward their work, toward their fellow men, and toward their employers. And it involves the equally complete mental revolution on the part of those on the management side— the foreman, the superintendent, the owner of the business, the board of directors—a complete mental revolution on their part as to their duties toward their fellow workers in the management, toward their workmen, and toward all of their daily problems. And without this complete mental revolution on both sides, scientific management does not exist.[8]

Taylor expected this "complete mental revolution" to bear several kinds of fruit:

1. Precise and systematic investigative procedures would replace intuitive judgments.
2. New perspectives, achieved through the application of scientific methods, would lead to more harmonious labor-management relations.
3. A spirit of industrial cooperation would develop.
4. Workers would strive to increase their output.
5. Each individual involved in the productive process would make every effort to develop his abilities in order to reach the common goals of maximum efficiency and prosperity.

While Taylor was explaining his theory of scientific management in the United States, in France Henri Fayol was analyzing the work of top management and administration[9]—an area largely unexplored by Taylor. Fayol described certain general principles—e.g., division of work, unity of command, stability of tenure—which he felt to be almost limitless in their application. He defined the principal management functions common to all levels of business, industry, or government as planning, organizing, commanding, coordinating, and controlling.

The works of Taylor and Fayol represent the first major stage in the development of management as a discipline—as a body of knowledge that could be organized and taught. Their work also forms the basis of what has been called the traditional view of administrative theory, which Gordon defines as follows:

---

[8] Frederick Winslow Taylor, in testimony before a special committee of the U.S. House of Representatives, 1916. Quoted by John F. Mee, *Management Thought in a Dynamic Economy* (New York: New York University Press, 1963), p. 40–41.

[9] See Henri Fayol, "General Principles of Management," in *Classics in Management,* edited by Howard F. Merrill (New York: American Management Association, 1960), pp. 217–241.

> Administration is treated more as a technical problem to be solved
> on a highly rationalized and programmed basis with formal arrange-
> ments and guidelines. The ends are frequently taken as given; means
> are to be engineered to produce desired outcomes with maximum
> efficiency. Fundamental ideas include those of hierarchy, authority,
> function, specialization, measurement, and efficiency.[10]

The first serious challenge to this concept of the manager and
the management function came in the 1920's, as a result of experi-
ments conducted by the Western Electric Company at its Haw-
thorne plant in Cicero, Illinois. The findings led to the development
of what has become known as the human relations theory of management. The project came to the public's attention in 1928, when
a group from the Harvard School, headed by Professor Elton Mayo,
were engaged as consultants. The publication of their definitive
report[11] marked the beginning of a new era in management theory
and practice. It revealed, for instance, that a simple physical or
engineering approach was totally inadequate for the motivation of
workers. It also established that in every large organization there
were small, informal social and informational networks which the
more formal hierarchical approach to organization had failed to
recognize.

In the ensuing twenty years industry has become increasingly at-
tentive to the work of social and behavioral scientists. The work
of Kurt Lewin first at the University of Iowa, then at MIT in the
late 1940's, for example, on group dynamics and on the use of
topological methods in the analysis of social structure has been
immensely fruitful. He has been followed by others such as Rensis
Likert and his colleagues at the University of Michigan, who have
reported on the comparative efficiency of similar groups working
under different forms of supervision—democratic and authoritarian;
Mason Haire at the University of California, who has been concerned with the organizational relationships of size, shape and
function; and Chris Argyris at Yale, who has been exploring the
conflict between organizational structure and individual effectiveness. At MIT the work continued under the stimulus of Douglas
McGregor on the application of motivational concepts to manage-

---

[10] Paul J. Gordon, "Transcend the Current Debate on Administrative Theory,"
Academy of Management Journal, VI, 4 (December 1963), (Bloomington, Indiana:
Indiana University Press), p. 290.

[11] F. J. Roethlisberger and W. J. Dickson, *Management and the Worker* (Cambridge: Harvard University Press, 1939).

ment philosophy. The further development of research and programs in group dynamics has been largely centered in the National Training Laboratories of the National Education Association headed by Leland Bradford. The studies of Herbert A. Simon, Richard A. Cyert and others at Carnegie Institute of Technology have further reshaped much of our understanding of administrative behavior in government and in industry.

Present-day advances in management theory and practices are based on innovations introduced in the 1950's—new concepts of quantitative analysis and of decision-making, new forms of adult education as exemplified in the university programs for executives at Harvard, Columbia and MIT, new concepts of work, and new designs for the organization of work. According to Bernard J. Muller-Thym, it was a time in which industry became aware of practices that "challenged successfully almost the total pre-existing practice."

The 1960's are apparently to be a decade of consolidation and elaboration. As yet there is no overarching theory of organization and administration which draws together the various schools and approaches. Lacking such a unified conceptual structure, there is increasing willingness to adopt a pluralistic approach to management problems.

Large industry and training needs. Over the past century big business has been becoming bigger and its structure more complex. One inevitable result has been the establishment of formal training programs for workers and managers, i.e. many firms with the more significant programs usually to be found in the larger companies.

First of all, there is the fact that with greater numbers of people in the organization the initial education and training of people to understand company operations, values and objectives becomes more important and, at the same time, dependent upon the performance of a functional education group. In a smaller company the top managers could directly communicate with the new employees, introducing them into company policies and practices. Thus one principal factor in growth, as it affects education in business and industry is the demand for programs of orientation and basic corporate policy training.

Sheer size also introduces a factor of complexity in industry education inasmuch as educational activities must be run at various locations throughout the country, covering within each location a wide variety of background, skills, and work assignments. The question of geographic dispersion and increasing size leads to a need for centralized educational planning and budget.

Influence of R&D

A final consideration, as a result of the growth of the American corporation, is increasing dependence upon technological investment.

The emphasis of the 1960's is on research and development (R&D). The most advanced education programs are found in those industries which have the highest investment in R&D. Over 90 per cent of the dollars invested for R&D in 1961 was accounted for by 300 companies with the largest R&D programs. These firms employ over half the scientists and engineers in industry *and* maintain the highest level of education and training activity. If R&D is considered an index of technological activity and the causative agent in developing requirements for education and training programs, then the number of R&D scientists employed per total number of employees in a given company will be related to that company's requirements for education and training investment. For as the scientist develops new devices or creates new processes, manufacturing procedures will have to be changed to accommodate the new concepts; and technicians and workers will have to be trained in the new procedures. This change radiates through the sales and other management functions of the organization. The following demonstrates the concentration of such talent.

> The aircraft and missiles industry ranked the highest with a ratio of 101 R&D scientists and engineers per 1000 employees. Other industries with particularly high ratios were scientific and mechanical measuring instruments (65); communication equipment and electronic components (64); drugs and medicine (51); and other electrical equipment (43). The lowest ratio reported was that in the textiles and apparel industry, which maintained an average staff of three R&D scientists and engineers for every 1000 employees.[12]

There would thus seem to be a correlation between technological capability—that is, R&D investment—and the general level of innovation and employment within an industry. Those industries which have the highest unemployment figures and the greatest economic difficulties are generally those in which the average educa-

---

[12] National Science Foundation, *Research and Development in Industry 1961.* (Washington, D.C.: U.S. Government Printing Office, 1964.)

tional level of the work force and the ratio of R&D scientists to total number of employees is lowest.

In recognition of this relationship between R&D investment and economic well-being, the federal government is actively encouraging the diffusion of technological change and training into those industries which suffer from a low rate of economic growth, especially through the activities of the Institute for Applied Technology within the National Bureau of Standards which was established in January 1964. This is not to suggest that educational programs and R&D expenditures will of themselves guarantee economic health; but it is significant that R&D investment and manpower development seem to go hand in hand with satisfactory levels of growth and employment.

CHAPTER II

Education in Business and in School:
A Comparison

As the educational activities of business expand both in size and in purpose, they begin to encounter many of the problems which have traditionally beset public and higher education. A purpose of this discussion is to compare the policies and practices developed in education in business and industry with those found in the schools. It is important to understand that the types of problems both face are, paradoxically, at once diametrically opposed and essentially the same.

The differences arise from the fact that education in the schools has a long history of philosophies, practices, and critical analyses. Education in business, on the other hand, has developed pragmatically, according to the needs and within the boundaries posed by circumstances. Furthermore, education in the schools exists as a separate, readily identifiable entity in society; as such, it is the object of constant concern and evaluation by the community as a whole. Its purposes are those of the community, and its success is measured in terms established by the society. Educational programs in business, most of which have developed within the confines of a particular firm or corporation, do not benefit from this general public concern. The purposes of business education vary with those of the different programs and organizations, and their success is measured along considerably less elastic scales—profitability, revenue growth, share of the market, and so on.

Despite these differences, however, education—whether in business or in the schools—is faced with the problem of making decisions in three vital areas: *content, values,* and *administration.* These areas are crucial for they determine the shape and direction of the educational program. Further, they assume prior decisions and directions as to the philosophy and purpose of the educational process itself. In public and higher education such decisions are made against a background of educational philosophy, traditional curriculum considerations and financial constraints imposed by the community. There is a continuing dialogue between professional educators and laymen which results in an expression, however imprecise, of the importance and role of the school to the society. Such a background for the educational problems in business and industry does not exist and the formulation of decisions in these areas is still a difficult process. So important is education in business and industry to society as a whole, however, that it will be of considerable advantage to society to bring to bear upon such educational programs all the experiences and insights of the educational community.

New Concepts of the Business Organization

As business and industrial firms have grown in size and importance they have come to be recognized as special "complete social" or "sub-government" units. Introducing new members into such organizations is a function analogous to the role traditionally played by education.

Throughout much of history, education—public or private—has been the agency for introducing the young person into the society and giving him an understanding of the society's values, mores and goals. Indeed, some educational philosophers believe that the school systems should not only conserve past experience and provide the training for future civic and social participation, but that the school itself should become an instrument for effecting social change.

In a sense, the large business corporation is faced with questions somewhat similar to those posed in public education. Educational activities in business, like education in the school, are used to bring the individual to an acceptance of new (to him) values. It may well be that the results of such activities, particularly in the area of management development, will eventually shape the future of the organization.

Before the turn of the century, the business organization was generally one which, to use Elton Mayo's phrase, constituted "an established society." A principal concern of business management in operating training programs was to provide the worker with a period of orientation to the firm. In this period, the worker learned his proper role in relation to the organization and to his fellow workers, the personnel policies of the company, and the minimum standards he would be expected to meet. The values of the organization, its rules and regulations, and the expectations of management were subject to little change; the worker was able to absorb them within a relatively short period early in his career, and needed little or no follow-up training later.

Today, however, the typical industrial concern constitutes what may be described as "an adaptive society." It is composed of individuals of different origins and even more varied educational and social backgrounds. The mobility characteristic of the present-day American society means that individuals may move from job to job almost at will; thus the composition of a given organization—and, with it, its values and purposes—are constantly changing. Whereas a nineteenth-century business firm emphasized its stability of values and employee loyalty, the modern organization places highest importance on the worker's ability to adapt to modifications of all kinds—whether these involve technological innovations in the work process, changes in personnel, or revisions of company policies and purposes.

Orientation courses still comprise a basic part of the training process, but they are enormously amplified and enhanced by intracompany communications of all kinds. House organs, company demonstrations and displays, meetings, seminars, and other devices are used to keep the worker continually aware of the company's goals. One organization regularly distributes more than twenty different house organs (planned according to plant location, company divisions, and employee functions), which are designed to keep employees, and their families, informed of the company's programs and progress. Nor is this particular example unique in the business world of today. Every major company has a wide network of communication and information, the purpose of which is to help the employee understand and accept management objectives and to provide a forum in which the employee may air his views, raise questions of general interest, and make suggestions of his own. Such an information program may seem to be of minor importance, in view of the day-to-day competitive pressures of the contemporary business environment. Actually, however, this is not the case: an effective system of intracompany communication and information is an essential aspect of business education and training. It is crucial to the vital relationship between management and employees as well as between business and the society as a whole.

Problems of Content

General education vs. technical training. While the nature of the productive process remained relatively stable over long periods of time, new members of the work force were able to learn their trade or craft through an extended apprenticeship or on-the-job training. Because the productive process remained constant, the new worker had only to learn the specific skills and procedures involved in his particular task. Today, however, the rate of technological innovation is such that knowledge of a specific set of skills and procedures will no longer serve the individual throughout his working life. The modern worker must have the mental ability and educational background that will make it possible for him to transfer his acquired knowledge to new work situations and to acquire new knowledge as the need presents itself.

This new responsibility of the worker poses a corresponding responsibility for management. The educational activities of the modern business organization must comprise more than a training program designed to transmit a set of specific technical skills. Because the nature of work is shifting from a blue-collar to a white-collar orientation, the demand for generalized educational training is becoming more persistent. The person who has received a well-rounded general education is in a better position to move with the company and to attain individual success. In view of the fact that the educational process must continue after the individual assumes a working career, it is imperative that part of the process of education within business and industry encompass at least part of a program of general education.

There is an important distinction between training and education. The purpose of *training* is to develop certain automatic facilities as in languages, bookkeeping, and the operation of machines. The function of *education,* however, is to provide the student with a capacity for analyzing and solving problems that confront him in his occupation, in his society, and within himself. It should also develop in him a desire to continue with intensive and systematic investigations after his formal program is completed. In the *training* program formulas and techniques are learned, rules are memorized, and mental or physical skills are developed through practice and repetition. In a genuine *educational* program, however, students concentrate on processes of analysis whereby they attain levels of generality, proficiency, and understanding which enable them to think intelligently in several fields even though they may not have had training in the detailed knowledge of any of them.[1]

Educational activities in business have thus assumed many functions in addition to those of training and orientation: They are now involved in the process of general education. Like officials of public and higher education, those responsible for education within the business community must now relate their programs—along with their goals, values, and problems—to the goals of the corporation and of the society as a whole.

The problem of content, for an educational program in business, therefore involves choices between a program of technical training and one of general education. Obviously, a training program geared to specific current needs involves less expense and produces measurable results far more quickly. Those who hold the purse strings in education, whether it be in business or in the schools, are more apt to approve of this type of program than one which includes what they are fond of describing as "frills" or "generalities."

An example of this problem occurs in the machine field. An individual may be trained to service machines by being taught the specific technology and processes associated with each type of machine. Then, as new machines are developed, he can be trained in the technology and processes of each new type. Under this system, the individual has no opportunity—and no ability—to build on past knowledge. This system does not take advantage of the fact that conceptually similar functions are performed differently on different types of machines. In a general education program, the individual would master both the conceptual and the functional aspects of machine design. With this knowledge he would be able to approach each newly developed type of machine, using his past training—both conceptual and specific—as a basis upon which to build his new capability. Furthermore, in such a training program it is possible to train workers in the servicing of new machines which may combine in different ways the functions which were separately performed in the past. By understanding the nature of each function and its several implementations in different technologies, the worker can achieve a maximum synthesis of knowledge with a minimum of repetition in instruction. The cost of a "conceptual" program is undeniably higher in the short run. By making this investment, however, one company was able to move through

---

[1] Walter Buckingham, *The Impending Educational Revolution* (Washington, D.C.: National Education Association, EIA, October 1961), p. 15.

three major technological revolutions in its product line and a multitude of different market applications at a total cost far lower than it would have been had each new stage required the retraining of its production and service forces.

Remedial education.   Another aspect of general education programs involves such subjects as arithmetic, reading, and basic science. These subjects would seem to have even less direct applicability than does conceptual training. Their inclusion in a company educational program, however, serves several necessary functions.

One plant, part of a large company, was faced with a major technological change in its product line. If the machinists and mechanical assembly workers were to become proficient in the new technology, they would have to be exposed to a program of remedial education. There was some concern that the expenditure of money and resources for such a program would be unjustifiably high. There were three alternatives: to reorganize the technological process into a series of simpler steps which could be performed by the workers at their current level of training; to dismiss the present workers and hire new workers skilled in the new technology; or to forego the new technology altogether. The first choice would have brought production costs to far too high a level; the second would have raised a serious and widespread problem of morale; the third —in a competitive business environment—might have been suicidal.

The company therefore decided to go ahead with the remedial education program. Well in advance of the proposed change-over, the management introduced instruction in arithmetic, algebra, reading, and writing—on company time and (optionally) on the workers' own time. Those workers who participated in the program were able to make the transfer to the new type of work which followed the introduction of the new technology. Thus this program proved to have very profitable and directly applicable results—but only after two or more years had elapsed. If, in cases of this nature, decisions are based on the short-run considerations of educational expense and lost worker time, the over-all company operation may be inhibited for several years and attractive market opportunities lost.

Not all company decisions to introduce programs of remedial general education are based on such dramatic circumstances, but the motivation behind the decision is essentially the same. Many companies offer, at company expense, courses in mathematics, English, physics, and other subjects. Some of these programs are offered during working hours; others are made available on the workers' own time. A recent National Education Association study proposed that four hours in the forty-hour work week be used for upgrading workers' skills or providing them with the means for general self-improvement.

The clerk who takes a course in mathematics and the secretary who takes a course in speed reading will turn in a better job performance. Thus the cost of such training is justified as an investment in their potential development. The educational investment is also justified if considered as an individual consumption item, for the worker benefits by becoming a more well-rounded person, bringing more understanding to—and deriving more fulfillment from—the duties and responsibilities of his job.

Those who oppose company programs of remedial or general education argue that such educational activity represents a misuse of stockholders' funds and a usurpation of the role of public and higher education. The first objection might be contested by pointing out that the stockholder's primary concern is profit; this being the case, any program designed to raise the company's profits— even over the longer run—is justified.

The example already cited provides ample illustration of the profitability of such a program. Workers whose innate abilities have been developed will ultimately turn in a better work performance, thus increasing the company's productivity and, ultimately, its profits. The second point is also open to argument. Certainly business organizations should avoid offering a complete range of courses, particularly in the fields of social science, psychology, political science, or other areas which involve questions of ethics or religious beliefs. But business management officials and professional educators have a common concern for, and a common stake in, the over-all educational level in the society. A worker today must be able to comprehend simple directions, perform elementary calculations, write concise memoranda, fill in complicated work forms, and perform hundreds of other similar tasks which occur daily in the modern business world. A remedial education program raises the morale of the worker by making it possible for him to avoid being replaced by someone of a higher skill level and, by raising his morale, it also increases his loyalty to the company and his total productive contribution. Rather than usurping the role of the schools, business and professional education have a common need to develop better techniques for the remedial training that will help to accomplish the objectives of the society as a whole.

Research and teaching. Business, like higher education, faces a major problem: How shall content reflect the most advanced knowledge in the field? In business, as in higher education, it is often difficult to persuade those who are doing the most advanced research in a given area to interrupt their investigations long enough to communicate their findings to those who might profit from such instruction.

Lecture and seminar series are planned to permit outstanding practitioners to share with others in the field their particular insights and competencies. The use of films and closed-circuit television can also be tremendously helpful. Nevertheless, the problem of bringing people with advanced knowledge into the classroom remains a major problem for education in business and in the schools.

Methodology. Who is to teach in the classroom? What should his background be? What competencies should he possess? These questions are as relevant to business as they are to professional education. Generally, education and training in business are conducted by people drawn from the organization itself. Such people usually lack professional teaching experience, and few companies have attempted to provide teacher training for members of the educational staff. If educational activities in business are to render their maximum potential, some provision must be made to allow those who will assume the teaching role to acquire a knowledge of modern teaching methods, devices, and practices.

Provision must also be made, as it is in the schools, for the teacher to refresh his knowledge of his particular field and to acquaint himself with the findings of the most recent research. In one company, individuals assigned to the educational program are periodically transferred to gain experience in the actual working environment. They return to their teaching tasks with a better understanding of their subject matter and a revitalized competency in their technical specialty. Only by constant attention to the quality of the teaching staff and by the development of firm programs for occasional work experience will management insure that what is being taught is of maximum value to the workers and to the company.

The educator in the business world is often as reluctant to introduce new teaching devices, such as audiovisual aids or programmed instruction, as are those working in other educational spheres. Business, however, has an unusual opportunity to employ the most advanced forms of educational technology. First, the subject matter dealt with more often falls into the factual and logical organization so important in programmed learning. Secondly the educational process in the business world deals only with adults, so that the motivation to learn may be considered to be higher than that of children in school. Because he is dealing with adults, the teacher need feel little compunction about trying out a new method. If it fails, he can always try another. Such a failure in an elementary school classroom, for instance, might irreparably damage a child's future attitudes and abilities. Finally, within the business enterprise the cost of innovative technology such as teaching machines, elegant audiovisual techniques, etc., may be more easily substantiated because of the general underlying investment philosophy. Attempts to keep the human resources of a corporation "in good repair" and to make them of greater value are in concert with the typical management approach to the protection and development of its physical resources and tools.

The business educator must also learn to make his own evaluations and to exercise his own judgment concerning the value of any particular practice or technique. The public school teacher may turn to a host of professional associations, school boards, and local experts for measurements, theories, and practices against which he may gauge the correctness of his solution to a particular problem. The business educator stands almost alone. He is dealing with an amorphous, pervasive function, and there is no professional association, no state body, and no group of experts to which he can appeal for help.

Values

A second major parallel between education in business and education in the schools involves the aims and objectives of the educational process. In this period, when the society places major value on education, it is inevitable that there should be great controversy over the purposes and goals of the educational system. And as educational activities in the business would grow in size and in complexity, a similar debate has arisen over the ends and objectives of the educational program in industry.

Educational environment. The learning environment is as important to the adult worker as it is to the school child. An atmosphere of negativism will decrease the worker's ability to function well in a specific training assignment. His level of function will also be affected by his attitude toward the company, his fellow workers, and the educational program itself. Just as the child is encouraged to learn if he feels that his parents value education, so the worker is encouraged to participate fully in educational programs if he feels that management and the company as a whole respect and believe in the principle of the self-improvement of the individual.

Some companies express the value they place on education through articles in house organs, through advertising, and through the daily behavior of managerial personnel. These companies increasingly emphasize top management's responsibility in expressing the organization's concern for the worker as an individual and for his maximum success within the company. These attitudes are not based on pure altruism, nor are they so presented; they are based on the realization that the development of human potential within the organization will result in maximum profit for the workers as individuals and for the company as a whole.

Commitment to lifelong learning. The society today views a lifelong commitment to learning as crucial to its survival in a nuclear age. The same commitment is essential to the modern corporation if it is to survive in the competitive environment. The business firm must not only endorse such a commitment, it must display it and encourage it. Methods should be formulated to recognize employee achievement in the company's training and educational programs. Just as a community displays the value it places on education by developing a superior school system, so does a company indicate the depth of its commitment by expanding and deepening its educational program and encouraging the participation of its employees.

Transmission of values. One of the important aspects of any educational process is the transmission of values by the teacher to the students. These values are conveyed not only through books but through the teacher's attitude, his language and figures of speech, and the illustrations he chooses. The corporation's image and goals will be profoundly affected by the people it chooses to carry out its educational program. Just as the community has difficulty articulating its goals and purposes, so the corporate organization often fails to provide the proper guidance and leadership through its educational activities. It is important that the teachers fully understand the nature and objectives of the organization. Their transmission of these values cannot be assured by the imposition of an arbitrary and rigid set of teaching procedures; rather, it must grow out of their own commitment to the idea of education and their own understanding and acceptance of the company's goals.

The individual and the organization. The aim of any educational process is to enable the learner to take his place as a functioning member of a social organization. This is a most difficult task, and one likely to arouse controversy. Educators must choose or alternate between conflicting goals: conformity or creativity, equality or excellence, stability or change. Perhaps the leading problem of the modern age will involve the individual's role in the various larger organizations of which he is a part. This problem finds a major manifestation in the business world, where the current concern is for the role of the individual in and toward the corporation.

The question of the individual's treatment of his divided loyalties is a principal consideration of any educational program. Because of the increasingly abstract nature of work and the interchangeability of people engaged in the process, the value of any job as a principal defining mechanism for questions of life value is diminishing. It follows from this that the worker's relationships and status will derive from his participation in a multiplicity of organizations. Within the corporation, for example, the engineer belongs to a specific engineering laboratory, to a professional discipline, to the local community, to the corporation, and so on. Such multifaceted group association can be a source of great strength for the individual in resolving his relationship with the business world. Training programs which tend to general and broadening education strengthen the individual and thereby make him able to move more freely in the several organizations to which he must belong.

Every large business organization, and many small ones, are increasingly concerned with the problem of developing and encouraging creativity and self-assurance, particularly as part of the management and executive development program. But the company must also decide how much questioning of its established values and policies may be permitted as part of the educational process. The wise encouragement and direction of such questioning leads to a fuller self-development of the future leaders of the organization.

An additional problem of values is raised by the increasing use of the techniques and findings of the behavioral sciences in business educational and training programs. Wrongly used, such techniques as psychological testing, directive and nondirective counseling, and the like may lower morale, and create disenchantment and frustration among employees. There is a growing fear that the large corporation uses the behavioral sciences to manipulate "the little man." Management, therefore, has an obligation to consider seriously the ethical issues involved in the use of such techniques; the issues include questions concerning the philosophy of work, the relation of the individual to the organization, and the responsibilities of leadership.

It is not easy for the professional manager to operate comfortably in the consideration of these questions, for they involve matters of a subtle and delicate nature. Yet training courses in engineering or technical work, sales operations, or management development cannot take place in an environment of ethical or moral neutrality. The attitudes and the values held by the leadership of the organization will be reflected in the classroom. The concern for the individual and his equity in the organization, both financial and psychological, should inform the activities of all personnel and education managers. The use of such techniques as psychological and personality testing, appraisals and evaluative systems, and sensitivity training involve the relationship and rights of the individual vis-a-vis the organization.

Problems of this kind are met commonly in public and higher education. The use of testing and evaluation techniques in the public school system, the availability of school psychologists, and the concern with mental health are related to the concern for the relationship and adjustment of the individual to the organization. Within the public and higher education systems there are separate functions available for focusing upon the proper use of behavioral scientific techniques. The constant audit and review by administrators, professional peers and laymen, assure that such practices are in accord with the general desires and expectations of the community.

In the essentially authoritarian structure of business, however, application of such techniques without careful assessment of their affect can lead to problems of employee morale. The employee must feel he is being assessed and appraised fairly and by uniform methods. Otherwise the feelings of uncertainty and disloyalty are apt to become part of the employees make-up. On the other hand, revising the appraisal and assessment practices to purely mechanical standardization removes the humaneness from the business environment and causes the employee to suffer feelings of frustration and insecurity as he thinks of himself as a cog in a machine. The difficult balance between these opposing positions must be carefully thought out by personnel and education managers within the various functions of business.

Problems of Administration

In the society as a whole, education is considered to be a formal and separate process, the financing and administration of which can be treated as a series of discrete and precisely defined activities. Education in business, however, has come to be considered an integral part of the total enterprise. Yet its costs, in terms of funds and resources, represent a substantial expenditure which must be budgeted and distributed; and its importance to the organization requires that careful attention be given to its administration and control.

Accounting costs and measuring value.   Perhaps the most difficult administrative aspect of business education and training is the identification and accrual of educational expenses. The educational function is spread through many different departments—personnel, public relations, communications—as well as the formal educational and training programs. All these agencies contribute to the educational process, and to its cost. Furthermore, accounting methods which seek to ascribe costs to accounts related to the main purpose of the business carry both formal and informal education expenses as sub-accounts—if, indeed, they are identified at all. For instance, the salaries of newly hired trainees are treated as an educational expense; those of employees participating in advanced training programs are not. Then, too, some companies treat educational costs as an expense while others capitalize it in the cost of the product. Such intricacies of accounting compound the difficulty of measuring the cost of education in business. Thus it is generally difficult to obtain accurate estimates of the amounts actually being spent, or even uniform definitions of such expenses within a given organization. It is more than likely the expenditures for both formal and informal programs of education in business far exceed present estimates.

Various estimates have been made of the size and cost of education in business and industry. Professor Clark estimates that "more

than 75% of all large-scale industrial concerns have programs for
education and training."[1] A 1962 Department of Labor survey indicated that almost 50% of the workers employed by smaller firms
(400–500 employees) work for organizations which have training
programs. The percentage of employees involved in actual training
at any one time varied from 13 to 30%. Manufacturing organizations, for example, had 6% of their force in training.

With respect to the larger firms, the following estimate is given:

> "Thirty-five firms having 10,000 or more employees gave data on
> expenditures for in-company education and training. The amounts
> spent by each firm varied from $15,000 to over $15 million. Eight
> firms reported expenditures of over $1 million, and five of the eight
> reported expenditures of over $5 million per firm. If expenditures
> for out-of-company training were added to in-company expendi-
> tures, it is likely that a number of firms have budgets for education
> and training that are comparable in amount to fairly large colleges
> and universities."[2]

The Manpower Report of the President, in surveying the range
of education and training in industries whose employees come under the State Unemployment Compensation Programs indicates:

> Large firms were much more employee-training conscious than
> smaller ones. Seventy-six percent of those with 500 or more em-
> ployees provided for such training. At the time of the survey, some
> 2.6 million employees were participating in training programs.
> General Motors, for example, retrains 7,200 employees per year;
> Ford retrains 3,000 per year; and IBM each year retrains about
> 100,000 employees of its customers.[3]

The dollar value of such investments is difficult to estimate. One
report, issued by the Chase Manhattan Bank, estimates that the
cost of education of employees by business and industry is now at
the rate of $17 billion a year. This figure represents one-third the
cost of the formal education programs in American schools and
colleges. This report defined education in business as "formal programs and informal training which take place during business hours
or after work, in plants, offices, in-company or out-of-company
classrooms with instruction given by supervisors, training staff mem-

---

[1] *Automation and the Challenge of Change* (Washington, D.C.: National Education Association), p. 148.

[2] Oscar N. Serbein, *Educational Activities of Business* (Washington, D.C.:
American Council on Education, 1961), p. 9.

[3] *Manpower Report of the President* (Washington, D.C.: Government Printing
Office, March 1963).

bers or outside experts and teachers."[4] On the basis of investment the value of on-the-job training accumulated by persons in the labor force was estimated at $405 billion, which represented 70% as much as the estimated total of $650 billion already invested in the formal education of those now working. It is estimated that the annual rate of growth of education in business is proceeding at 5½% as opposed to the rate of 4½% for public and higher education.

Strangely enough, it may be the very difficulty involved in measuring its cost which may account for the spread of educational activity in business. In most organizations, it is only when educational reports are accrued and demonstrated on a consolidated accounting report that concern is generated over the "high cost" of education. Then, as is true in the case of public education when new taxes are levied, there are indignant demands to cut down expenses, eliminate "frills," and make other drastic curtailments. When the indignation subsides, effective educational activity resumes.

Teaching—administration: career paths.   Approximately half the companies engaged in educational activities draw their teaching staffs from within the organization itself—very often from among the younger members for whom the teaching function is part of their own training program. In some companies, for instance, sales training is carried on by a relatively permanent staff supplemented by younger salesmen with two or three years' experience. These younger men not only have the advantage of a more recent knowledge of the product, sales trends, and selling procedures, but they are also more "mobile"—that is, they can be assigned to different geographical areas according to the training needs of the company.

Many of the people chosen for top positions in business educational programs come from the personnel and marketing departments. They usually have had long experience with the company and with its objectives; they have an interest in and an understanding of training problems, and bring a practical approach to their solution.

The typical business education staff also includes a core of professional educators, people who have had experience in teaching and educational administration. These people generally are concerned with curriculum development, education research, and operation of plant and facilities.

---

[4] *Business in Brief* (New York: Chase Manhattan Bank, November 1962).

Finally, there are those staff members drawn from operating assignments. These are generally engineers or scientists who take on temporary teaching assignments to bring the technical staff up-to-date on current developments in their fields. Their activities are often supplemented by those of college and university teachers who join the staff as part-time consultants or teachers.

So varied an educational staff presents problems of motivation, reward, and evaluation. Professional members of the staff may feel frustrated by the fact that their performance is directed and evaluated by a management which has little or no educational background. Or they may feel thwarted when ideas and techniques they seek to introduce are measured against the business objectives of the firm. Finally, there is the danger that some of the individuals assigned to the educational program are those who had become "problem people" in other departments of the company, or whose careers had come to an effective standstill. Such a practice may have a devastating effect on staff morale.

An additional problem is the difficulty of bringing into a corporation, at an appropriately high level, educators of advanced experience and professional standing. Such people may be at a disadvantage in a business educational program, where education and training—placed as they are within the purposes and goals of the organization—are almost entirely dependent upon experience in company affairs.

A wise policy for business education involves keeping a careful staff balance among professional educators, temporarily assigned managers and younger personnel, and professional and technical consultants. Provision must also be made for teaching staff members to update their technical knowledge and skills at periodic intervals.

Policy and practice. The public school system is constantly concerned with the problem of the respective roles of the school board and the members of the administration in the determination and execution of educational policies. Usually, the board carefully articulates its policies and insists that they be implemented by the administration. A similar situation exists between the management of a company and its educational staff in regard to policies concerning education expense, recruitment and training, selection and training of teachers, educational research, extension of the curriculum, and operation of plant facilities. In each case, the management must evolve policies and objectives which are in line with the larger purposes and needs of the company as a whole. It is the duty of the administrators of the educational program to make sure that these policies are appropriately transmitted and executed.

Conclusions

These are but some of the many parallels between education in business and education in the schools. Because the enormous expansion of business educational activities has taken place over a relatively brief period, there has not yet developed the necessary degree of cooperation between the educators in the two fields. Such cooperation is most desirable, for it will make available to business and industry the experience, the knowledge, and the competency of the professional education community.

CHAPTER III

The Nature of Modern Business:
Problems and Goals

The Corporation as a Social Entity

The new need for education in business and industry springs from the change in the very nature of business in the modern world. The corporation, for example, is not merely a business organization; it is a new social entity—one which, again using Professor Mayo's phrases, constitutes "an adaptive rather than an established society."

> In the established societies of no more than a century ago, it was possible to assume a sufficient continuity of industrial processes, and therefore apprenticeship to a trade was the best method of acquiring skill, both technical and social. The technical skill required by industry in these days has developed in two directions. On the one hand, a much higher type of skill is required—that, namely, which is based upon adequate scientific and engineering knowledge and is consequently adaptable or even creative. On the other hand, the skill required of the machine-hand has drifted downward; he has become more of a machine tender and less of a mechanic.
> The skills acquired by the individual during apprenticeship . . . were in balance in respect of the situations he encountered. What was demanded of him technically did not require social skills of the order necessary to adjust to constantly changing work associates. Stability of techniques went hand in hand with stability in companionship.[1]

In an established society, the individuality of the young person is subordinated to the needs and practices of the group. Group attitudes and codes determine the social order and direction of his life. In such a society, knowledge is transmitted through direct learning and apprenticeship; any change in family career patterns is so slow as to be almost imperceptible. Furthermore, it is relatively easy for the individual to perceive the expectations of such a society, and his own role in it. In return for his assumption of that role—i.e.,

---

[1] Elton Mayo, *The Social Problems of an Industrial Civilization* (Andover, Mass.: The Andover Press, 1945), p. 13.

his commitment to the group—the society guarantees the individual a degree of stability and a measure of participation.

The adaptive society, on the other hand, is characterized by change—both in the society and in the individual's relation to it. The mobility of the individual within social groups, and the opportunity for individual development, are limited only by talent and by luck. But because this mobility is enjoyed by all the members of the group, the individual is faced with a constantly fluctuating set of social and business relationships. Thus he must learn to adapt to each new group, to perceive its expectations, and to take up his proper role in it.

One of the central causes of this social flux lies in the changed, and changing, nature of business:

- The growing size and internal complexity of business firms increases the difficulty of organization problems, diffuses the process of decision-making, and greatly increases the need for coordination and planning within the enterprise.
- Ownership and management have been separated in large firms, and salaried executives, picked for their managerial abilities rather than their wealth or family connections, have largely taken over business leadership.
- Rapid scientific and technological change requires a new and more professionally equipped group of managers—men with the technical background to communicate with scientists and engineers, to direct long-range planning, and to adjust all parts of a business to such revolutionary changes as automation and electronic data processing.
- Management has the increasingly complex task of maintaining good relations with its own employees, with labor organizations, with government, and with the broad public. American business is going increasingly international—and this adds new political, economic, social, and administrative complexities to management's tasks.[2]

Each of these factors has an impact, not only on the nature of business, but also on the nature of the society as a whole. It is the responsibility of management to help the individual worker to adjust to the new adaptive environment in which he finds himself, to make clear its expectations, and to help him assume his proper role.

The problem of size may be illustrated by pointing out that the "population" of some of the larger corporations—General Motors, for example, or U.S. Steel—is larger than that of the city of

---

[2] Leonard Silk, *The Education of Businessmen* (New York: Committee for Economic Development, December 1960), p. 9.

Florence at the peak of the Renaissance. This may help to indicate the awesome authority and concomitant responsibility which devolve upon the top management of the modern corporation. The orientation of new members in the corporate organization, the development of their professional and technical skills, the maintenance of a highly trained management staff, and the maximum development of each individual's potential—these are responsibilities managers must discharge in order to effect progress. The authority, power, and responsibility held in the corporation is not directly analogous to the political power held in other authoritarian systems; more often than not it rests on a consensus of a community of managers within the corporation. This consensus is often informally expressed and operative over long periods of time. Indeed one of the most difficult tasks in education in business and industry is articulating both the authority and responsibility of the organization, particularly as these are related to the individual's development and commitment to the organization.

And because the activities of the corporate giants affect every phase of American life in the twentieth century, the management of these organizations also has a responsibility toward the society as a whole. The group is a relatively small one. Of the 1.3 million corporations in the United States, the top 1000 produce 80 per cent of the goods and services consumed. The 7129 U.S. companies with 100 or more employees (2.5% of the nation's 286,817 manufacturing corporations) account for 90% of total manufacturing assets and 83% of total sales. The nation's top 13 employers, firms with 100,000 or more workers, have assets of $37.9 billion (15.3% of total U.S. manufacturings assets) and sales of $47.1 billion (13.6% of total sales).[3] Even in 1952 it could be written that,

> General Motors . . . today spends more money annually than the United States government used to spend in the 1920's (even including the expenses of the Army and Navy). Nearly half of all gainfully employed Americans are on the payroll of a corporation; if we exclude farmers and other self-employed people from our reckoning, the proportion is much larger.[4]

On a more personal level, almost every family in America has one or more persons who work or have worked with an American corporation.

---

[3] "12,000 Leading U.S. Corporations," *News Front*, p. 7.
[4] Frederick Lewis Allen, *The Big Change—America Transforms Itself* (New York: Harper & Row, 1952), p. 75.

The increases in the population of these corporations over the past 20 years are indicated by the record of a few typical organizations, as drawn from annual reports. (See Table I.)

TABLE I

POPULATION GROWTH OF REPRESENTATIVE CORPORATIONS

		1935	1945	1950	1955	1960
AT&T	Employees	241,169	387,300	523,251	615,895	580,405
GM	Employees	211,712	345,940	465,239	624,011	595,151
IBM	Employees	8,654	18,527	30,261	56,421	104,241

Figures such as these reveal how large is the stake of the modern American corporation in the society. The responsibility assumed by business management must therefore be correspondingly large—in self-protection, if for no other reason. In its treatment of employees, stockholders, and the general public, management must demonstrate a sincere concern for the fair distribution of the fruits of corporate activities.

The history of the corporate organization, which dates back to the days of ancient Rome, is not uniformly impressive. The corporation was originally developed as a device for protecting family wealth in the event of the untimely demise of the head of the household. In the Middle Ages, it was made a legal institution and for several centuries thereafter was both used and abused by members of the European royalty.

> Speculation, dishonesty, and financial excesses caused the South Sea Bubble crash in 1720, and so discredited the corporation as an institution that for nearly one hundred years thereafter it was virtually outlawed in the English-speaking world. Grudgingly its use was resumed as the nineteenth century opened . . . As the century drew to its close, it had become a commercial instrument of formidable effectiveness, feared because of its power, suspect because of the extent of its political manipulations . . . admired because of its capacity to get things done.[5]

The image of the modern corporation has lost many of its menacing aspects—partly because government regulations now forbid the more flagrant abuses of economic powers and partly because the introduction of professional managers, who have a relatively small entrepreneurial stake in the organization, has given rise to a new sense of social and economic responsibility and a desire to

---

[5] Adolf A. Berle, in a foreword to Edward S. Mason, ed., *The Corporation in Modern Society* (Cambridge, Mass.: Harvard University Press, 1959).

develop a benevolent public image. So effective have these efforts been that, as Berle points out: "its position as a major method of business organization has been assured."[6] Not only has its position been assured, but the American corporation has also become a vital and positive contributor to our social, as well as economic, well-being.

Professionalism in the Corporation

As the responsibility of management has increased, there has developed the concept of business as a profession, to which Professors Gordon and Howell have given perceptive consideration. Accepting Follett's definition of *profession* as "a foundation of science and a motive of service," they go on to develop four criteria:

> First, the practice of a profession must rest on a systematic body of knowledge of substantial intellectual content and on the development of personal skill in the application of this knowledge to specific cases. Second, there must exist standards of professional conduct, which take precedence over the goal of personal gain, governing the professional man's relations with his clients and his fellow practitioners. . . . (Third), a profession has its own association of members, among whose functions are the enforcement of standards, the advancement and dissemination of knowledge, and, in some degree, the control of entry into the profession. Finally, there is a prescribed way of entering into the profession through the enforcement of minimum standards of training and competence.[7]

Gordon and Howell also point out the difficulty of applying these criteria to the business world:

> . . . unlike the traditional professions, the businessman's client is not clearly defined. First and foremost, a businessman's loyalty is to the enterprise with which he is associated, and the company can be taken to be his client. (In this sense, perhaps, we can speak of the motive of "service.") But a business enterprise can have a complex of objectives, only one of which is profits. . . . Are the businessman's goals of service and his standards of conduct to be geared solely to the objectives of the firm, or are there to be standards expressed in terms of the quality of the particular kind of service the individual contributes? And if there is a conflict of goals, how is *quality of service* to be interpreted?[8]

Although this conflict between "professionalism" and "profitabil-

---

[6] *Ibid.*
[7] R. A. Gordon and J. E. Howell, *Higher Education for Business* (New York: Columbia University Press, 1959), p. 69–70.
[8] *Ibid.*

ity" is very real, the new sense of social responsibility pervading the business world is aiding its satisfactory, though slow, resolution. This responsibility is manifested through the publication of annual financial reports, compliance with government regulations, description of productive processes, and exchanges of technical information both within the business environment and with the public at large. A certain element of secrecy (some may prefer to call it prudence) still surrounds the timing of announcements or of new market entries, but this is inevitable—and, perhaps, even desirable, in a free, competitive economy. Generally, however, it is acknowledged that the exchange and dissemination of information is a process highly beneficial to the over-all health of the American economy.

> . . . the most characteristic of all American institutions for the pooling of information are trade conventions. In 1930, according to *The Wall Street Journal,* there were 4000 trade associations in the United States; now . . . there are no less than 12,000—1500 national ones and 10,500 state or local ones. And so many of these organizations have salaried managers that . . . two hundred of the managers gathered in Chicago in 1951 to consult together as a trade association of managers of trade associations.[9]

It is not uncommon for representatives at these trade association conventions to conduct seminars in which the products and services of each company are analyzed and discussed. The representatives also view educational films explaining technical processes, watch closed-circuit television demonstrations of complicated equipment, and publish informational brochures for distribution to people within the industry and to the general public.

Trade associations are not the only forums for the exchange and dissemination of ideas and information; the number of professional associations has also increased within the past twenty years. There are literally thousands of such groups, ranging from the American Society for Corporate Secretaries and the National Association of Cost Accountants to the National Institute of Electrical Engineers, The Institute of Management Sciences, and the Society for Industrial and Applied Mathematics. At meetings of these societies, individual members present and discuss new ideas, processes, and techniques. The proceedings are published for the benefit of the industry and the public.

---

9 White, *op. cit.,* p. 245.

The Nature of Work

Although size and complexity are undeniably major factors in the changed nature of business, an even more crucial role has been played by those scientific and technological innovations which have served to change the very nature of work.

Adam Smith's description of the work process in a pin factory provided an indication of the specialization to come:

> One man draws out the wire, another straightens it, a third cuts it, a fourth points it, a fifth grinds it at the top for receiving the head; to make the head requires two or three distinct operations; to put it on, is a peculiar business, to whiten the pins is another; it is even a trade by itself to put them into the paper; and the important business of making a pin is, in this manner, divided into about eighteen distinct operations; . . .
>
> This great increase of the quantity of work, which, in consequence of the division of labour, the same number of people are capable of performing, is owing to three different circumstances; first, to the increase of dexterity in every particular workman; secondly, to the saving of the time which is commonly lost in passing from one species of work to another; and lastly, to the invention of a great number of machines which facilitate and abridge labour, and enable one man to do the work of many.[10]

The outstanding characteristic of the modern productive process is, then, specialization: the breaking down of the process into a series of discrete, relatively simple tasks. It is this concept which forms the basis for modern techniques of mass production. Each operation or work station may involve a complex of men and materials, but each is a definable and complete entity—linked, of course, to the other work stations which comprise the productive process. Because the cost of investment in such a process is high—involving specialized tools, worker training, and production planning—the principle aim in the theory of mass production is to make work stations as simple as possible, to keep the production line moving, and to turn out as many units as the market can absorb at a price profitable to the producer.

The increasing specialization of the work task requires an ever-rising level of skills on the part of the worker. In a modern machine assembly plant, for instance, even the semiskilled worker is expected to solve problems involving pattern recognition (e.g., in-

---

[10] Adam Smith, *The Wealth of Nations* (Chicago: The Great Books Foundation, 1955), pp. 6, 9.

serting small elements or sub-assemblies into larger units; watching meters, gauges, and other indicators), deviations from normal work flow (as when assembly-line materials are mispositioned or jammed), and matters of judgment (e.g., rearranging the order in which units are introduced into work stations). In addition, skilled workers are needed to maintain the machine shops, design rooms, and model shops which must be included in every automated factory.

It is clear, then, that the development of worker skill is, from the point of view of management, not only desirable but essential. Its importance increases when one considers the more dramatic changes that lie ahead as automation moves to include what may be called the rationalization of the control function.[11] In the now outdated version of the automatic production line, work schedules were established in one department, work operations were organized in a second, machines built or purchased in a third. Each department operated by itself, with only a minimal amount of interaction with the other two.

The modern production line is quite different. The total operations and work flow are now considered as a single system which may be rationalized and programmed.[12] Purchases of raw materials are related to market shipments and sales. Machine use and work load schedules are arranged so as to assure the optimum use of facilities.

The rationalization of the production process and the control function have been accompanied by the use of electronic and mechanical devices which can perform incredibly complex logical and mathematical operations. Further, through the use of high-precision mechanical equipment it is possible to duplicate with finer precision the motions of the human hand, transport at high speeds articles smaller than the head of a pin, and arrange for the manipulation of these entities into completed sub-assemblies.

By the same token, extremely cumbersome and power-consuming operations can be automated with equivalent delicacy of control. The modern rolling mill, engine manufacturing facility, or large petro-chemical cracking plant are examples of control and automation. In a sense we have extended the dimensions of man's

---

[11] The control function is that set of budgets, procedures, measurements, and reactions which govern the total flow of work through the plant.

[12] Operations are "rationalized" in that they are explicitly expressed in terms of functions which can be designed and engineered, and then arranged in appropriate sequences.

ability to see the final result, to exercise a range of power enormously beyond his own muscular ability, and to demonstrate motions which are at once more powerful and delicate than those of the most accomplished human hand. Such capability in extending the sensory domain leads to the development of machines which can integrate physical work and control functions into a single operating system.

The effect of all these developments is to remove the worker from direct involvement in much of the work process. Now that automated devices are available which can perform many mechanical tasks more quickly and more precisely than man possibly could, the role of the worker is to understand the mechanism of the device and to contribute to its operation his human intelligence, foresight, perception, and judgment.

> . . . technology has created a new relationship between man, his education, and his work, in which education is placed squarely between man and his work. Although this relationship has traditionally held for some men and some work (on the professional level, for example), modern technology has advanced to the point where the relationship may now be said to exist for all men and all work.[13]

Motivation, Evaluation and Reward

The difficulty of measuring the cost and value of educational programs in business and industry has already been discussed (see p. 25). This is part of the larger difficulty involved in the motivation, evaluation, and reward of all the work connected with the abstract world of modern science and technology. How large must an engineering staff be in order to produce efficiently? Is it worthwhile to incur the additional costs involved in communicating company policies to employees and the public? What is the value of an educational seminar for the managerial staff? What standard of measurement is to be applied to the contributions of long-range planners, financial analysts, marker researchers, or salesmen? The answers to these questions are, clearly, not easily found.

It is almost impossible to set an accurate value on the contributions of the so-called white-collar workers—and yet these workers (see Table II) now comprise more than 50 per cent of the American labor force.

---

[13] Grant Venn, *Man, Education, and Work* (Washington, D.C.: American Council on Education, 1964. Used by permission), p. 1.

TABLE II

EMPLOYED PERSONS, BY MAJOR OCCUPATION GROUP AND SEX
PERCENT DISTRIBUTION

	1963	1957	1948
White-collar workers	43.9	40.6	36.1
Professional, technical and kindred workers	12.0	9.9	6.7
Managers, officials, and proprietor, except farmers	10.6	10.3	10.7
Clerical and kindred workers	14.9	14.1	12.5
Sales workers	6.3	6.3	6.1
Blue-collar workers	36.3	38.3	40.4
Craftsmen, foremen, and kindred workers	13.0	13.3	13.7
Operatives and kindred workers	18.2	19.3	20.9
Laborers, except farm and mine	5.2	5.7	5.9
Service workers	13.1	11.7	10.2
Farm workers	6.7	9.3	13.3

MEDIAN YEARS OF SCHOOL COMPLETED BY THE EMPLOYED
CIVILIAN LABOR FORCE 18 YEARS OLD AND OVER, BY
OCCUPATION GROUP, COLOR AND SEX

	March 1962	March 1957	October 1948
OCCUPATION GROUP AND SEX			
Professional and managerial workers	13.9	13.3	12.8
Clerical and sales workers	12.5	12.4	12.4
Craftsmen, operatives, and laborers, except farm and mine	10.4	9.7	9.0

Source: U.S. Department of Labor, *Manpower Report of the President* and *A Report on Manpower Requirements, Resources, Utilization, and Training* (Washington, D.C.: USGPO, 1964).

The lack of direct physical connection with the work process and the lack of identification with a given piece of work which is typical of the white-collar worker leads not only to difficulties in measurement but also to personal frustration, alienation from the organization, and the breakdown of the human community formed by the corporation.

As a result, within the business community—and particularly in the graduate schools of business—increasing attention is being paid to organization theory and administrative practices. The problem is one of developing techniques through which the growing impersonalization of the work process may be counteracted by an increased personalization of the business environment. This is one of the basic concerns underlying management's increased preoccupation with educational activity.

Because the work process is less and less associated with physical labor or direct machine activity considerable thought has been applied to the problem of describing the "work" people do in terms of other dimensions. Since a man's work may not be capable of description in terms of machine rates, piece work or process variables it is natural to turn to other, often more vague, measures such as skills required, personal attitudes and characteristics, educational background, etc. Even where jobs are related to the machine process some of the same descriptors are used. This breaking down of the job into component parts reflects the application of the rationalized and "technical" approach which has been successful in the engineering of things.

Further, the resultant analysis and description of the job and its relationship can lead to a better planning of the human resources required and also the educational investment needed to develop these resources in the best possible manner.

A recent practice in American industry involves the development of job descriptions which outline the nature of each particular job, its relationship to other jobs, and the skills and educational background required for it. These descriptions are then organized into a job-skill inventory.

As products and services change, the combination of skills required to produce them will also change. By comparing skill inventories with skill requirements, management may continually revise and update its explicit statements of educational and training requirements. Comparison of skill inventories and skill requirements will also make it possible to plan and organize effective training and educational programs within the corporation. The difficulties of measurement are also lessened: standardized methods of testing employees against required skill levels are being developed and used with increasing frequency. Such testing procedures have several major advantages:

1. They identify those employees who need remedial assistance.
2. They identify those employees whose skill levels can be raised.
3. They provide guidelines for devising the most effective training programs.
4. They provide a greater and more equal opportunity for all employees to participate in impending production and service changes.

The increased use of data-processing techniques, standardized methods of testing and evaluation, and accurate job descriptions to undertake effective programs *are* designed to reconstitute and upgrade specific plant or technical populations. It can be seen, then, that the management of skills inventory carries with it the concepts of employee mobility, trainability, and motivation.

The effectiveness of skills inventory management has been demonstrated by one company, which has used the system both to upgrade its plant personnel and to introduce new products to its sales division. Each job in the plant is structured so that its description could be written in terms of standard skills. Personnel files outline the educational background and skill levels of each employee. New skill-level inventories, anticipating future technological and market developments, are then matched against existing skill levels. When the differences have been determined, adequate programs of remedial education or training are devised and employees are actively urged to participate in them. The net result of this activity is a low level of employee turnover, and a high level of morale and skill attainment.

The same company keeps separate records of its sales staff, each of which outlines the individual's educational status both before he joined the corporation and since. Before new products are put on the market, the records are examined to determine which salesmen will need upgrading. These men, selected on the basis of educational background, skill level, and current sales responsibilities, then participate in an advanced training program. The result, in this case, is a knowledgeable and effective sales performance.

The development of skill inventories within the corporate organization, their constant reappraisal and revision, and the development of effective remedial and advanced training programs assure the company that it is making maximum use of all its human resources. However, as we increase the use of formal mechanisms for maintenance of skill inventory, appraisal and evaluation systems, methods must be developed which will guarantee the rights of the individual with respect to the information about him which is recorded and with his stake in the "system." In the future this well may be a major area of concern in the managements of all of our large bureaucracies, government, business, the universities, and so on.

Education as Investment

A major factor governing the use of educational programs in business involves the concept of education as an investment, which, in turn, is based on the concept of the worker as a form of capital.

Perhaps the first, and certainly the most heroic, estimate of the money value of a human being to society is found almost three hundred years ago in the writings of the renowned British political arithmetician, Sir William Petty. In 1687, for example, Petty estimated that a resident of England was worth a solid £90, while an Irishman was worth only £70. . . .

And in 1862, J. T. Rogers . . . argued that it is "unphilosophical to ignore capital in the person of a laborer and to recognize it in a machine." . . . So the thoughts that guide contemporary efforts in this field are not new. What is new is the weaving of the human capital factor into the fabric of economic development—into its theory, policy, and practice.[14]

The notion of treating education itself as a form of human capital owes much of its current popularity to Professor Theodore Schultz, of the University of Chicago who writes:

Since education becomes a part of the person receiving it, I shall refer to it as *human capital*. Since it becomes an integral part of a person, it cannot be bought or sold or treated as property under our institutions. Nevertheless, it is a form of capital if it renders a productive service of value to the economy. The principal hypothesis underlying this treatment of education is that some important increases in national income are a consequence of additions to the stock of this form of capital. Although it will be far from easy to put this hypothesis to the test, there are many indications that some, and perhaps a substantial part, of the unexplained increases in national income in the United States are attributable to the formation of this kind of capital.[15]

Over recent years, it has come to be recognized that education plays an important part in increasing the gross national product and raises the standard of living. The increase in gross national product over the past fifty years, for example, has exceeded expectations based on the normal stock of tangible capital and manhours worked. This excess (which economists estimate as one-half to one-third the increase in output) may be properly attributed to the higher educational level of the work force. Furthermore, the role of education in increasing national output appears to be growing more significant:

---

14 Walter Heller, "Men, Money, and Material," *The Educational Record*, XLIV, 1 (Washington, D.C.: American Council on Education, January 1963), p. 12. Used by permission.

15 Theodore W. Schultz, "Capital Formation by Education," *The Journal of Political Economy*, LXVIII, 6 (Chicago, Illinois: University of Chicago Press, December 1960), p. 571.

We now know, for instance, that less than half the rise in this country's output since 1960 can be accounted for by increased amounts of labor and capital. The rest, it appears, has come largely from improved skills and education of the labor force and from advances in management and technology.[16]

Nor are these theories without basis in actual statistics: those firms which have grown fastest in profits, dollar sales, population, or contribution to society have been those which invested most in science and technology and in the development of their human potential.

Economists have traditionally treated education as an item of consumption—i.e., its cost is treated as a current expense and the item itself does not contribute to an increase in wealth. This is the view that obtains in public and higher education. Thus administrators in these fields are faced with the problem of having to justify educational expense as an on-going annual problem. If the new view of education as capital investment were to gain wide acceptance, the public sector could then make heavier long-range investments in the educational plant with the assurance of an increased "return": a larger gross national product and a higher standard of living. The same reasoning applies to educational investment by business and industry. For, as Eckaus points out:

> From the viewpoint of the individual and of society as a whole, . . . education is similar to the production of physical capital goods. Both require the use over a period of time of facilities such as buildings, materials, and equipment, and labor skills. Both necessitate the sacrifice of goods and services that might otherwise have been produced. Both will yield "services" over some subsequent period. . . .
> . . . There is no generic term for the developmental efforts that must be applied to natural resources to make them into productive capital, but there is such a term for efforts to develop human resources. It is *education*.[17]

If, as appearances indicate, one-third to one-half of the increase in national productivity is the result of advances in science and technology and their knowledgeable application to the productive process, then it behooves the large corporations—which have the largest stake in the future of the national economy—to make a crit-

---

[16] Luther Hodges, *Growth Through Technology* (Washington, D.C.: U.S. Department of Commerce, 1963).

[17] Richard S. Eckaus, "Education and Economic Growth," *Higher Education as an Investment in People* (Washington, D.C.: U.S. Department of Health, Education, and Welfare, 1962), p. 103.

ical assessment of the potential contribution of educational investment to corporate growth.

Nearly all corporations of the size considered in this discussion use formal planning mechanisms—to assess market developments and technological innovations and to anticipate requirements for plant and facility investment and human skill development. Effective corporate planning must take into account the cost of a continuing program designed to match technical and professional skills to the abstract work process. Few companies today are making maximum use of formal and informal educational and training programs as an approach to the problem of corporate growth. Education and training can increase the rate of growth of the corporation, just as it has the economic growth of the nation.

A specific problem in the management of education as an investment by the corporation is the development of an accurate schedule of the true costs of educational activity. As has been pointed out (see p. 24), because of its pervasiveness, educational activity is normally distributed as an expense, often hidden under different names in the various departments and functions of the organization. The acceptance of the concept of education as an investment would almost certainly lead to more sophisticated methods of accounting and financial control for this intangible aspect of the business operation.

Certainly such a development is more likely now than it would have been at a time when the physical work process was considered to be of paramount importance and the white-collar "intangible" function was relegated to a relatively minor position. As the effects of technology and science on industry become more pronounced, the work process will become increasingly rationalized and a greater transferability of general skills will be required of an ever larger group of people. As these developments occur, it will become increasingly necessary for business to organize a sensible control system for the real and intangible costs involved in the management and development of its human potential. The formation of such a system will emphasize the significance of education and training to business management, and strengthen its role in the community as a whole.

Leadership Development

One function traditionally associated with the educational process is the development of leadership and the transmission of cultural values. In business, the problem of leadership development is compounded by the fact that the members of the "community" are not bound together by a common allegiance to a particular flag, church, or race. The loyalty of the members of a business organization is measured by the depth of their commitment to the work they are doing and by the inherent value they perceive in it. The attitude of the individual toward his job has gained in significance over the past few decades, for increasingly the job has come to be viewed as an index of his position and status in the society. And, of course, now as always the job is the visible proof of the individual's entrance into the adult world and his acceptance by that world. Here the job "association" is of much more importance than the job "content."

> A man's occupation in American society is now his single most significant status-conferring role. Whether it be high or low, a job status allows the individual to form some stable conception of himself and his position in the community.
> . . . a job becomes the symbol of acceptance into the adult world. Neither religious ceremonies (which come too early), nor marriage (which for many comes too late), nor school graduation ceremonies (a good excuse for some new clothes and a round of parties) ranks even close to the job as an initiation symbol.[18]

The new social and emotional significance which attaches to the job and more importantly to his "association" with an organization now makes of the concept of job-holding something more than the mere notion of "earning a living." It is essential that management recognize this deep psychological involvement on the part of their employees.

This involvement emphasizes the importance of educational activities in business, for it is through such activities that the values and attitudes of the organization are transmitted and internalized. Far more important than formal learning materials to the transmission of these values is the attitude of the teacher and of management toward the entire concept of education and self-improvement.

> Perhaps the greatest of all pedagogical fallacies is the notion that a person learns only the particular thing he is studying at the time. Collateral learning in the way of formation of enduring attitudes, likes and dislikes, may be and often is much more important. . . . The most important attitude that can be formed is that of desire to go on learning. . . .[19]

---

[18] Venn, *op. cit.*, pp. 11, 12.
[19] John Dewey, *Experience and Education* (New York: Collier Books, 1963), p. 96.

Dewey's concept of collateral learning is as important to the corporation as it is to the classroom. This was stressed by the report of two major surveys of the educational activities of a business organization by consultants drawn from the fields of public and higher education. The report emphasized the importance of:

1. The transmission of intangible values as part of the formal training process.
2. The proper selection, training, and supervision of teachers.
3. The articulation of the company's basic philosophies and policies by specific top management officials in order that these might be integrated into the formal training program.

This emphasis on the transmission of values is an argument not for propagandizing or brainwashing, but for the clear articulation and presentation of company goals. Only if the employees thoroughly understand the basic policies and goals of the organization will their criticisms, suggestions, and expressions of personal attitudes— so actively encouraged by many corporations—have constructive value.

The transmission of attitudes and values assumes even more importance at the managerial and executive levels. For example a major problem which might be considered in executive and management development is the question of corporate loyalty vs. personal conscience. For instance, the sales management of a large corporation dominant in one field must not use the size and success of the corporation to stifle or thwart the efforts of smaller competitors. In some industries, the problem of intercompany protective or collusive price fixing has been a major concern. These are issues which might arise out of an overzealous interpretation of the concept of corporate loyalty, and which might in turn give rise to a crisis of personal conscience.

The company's definition of *corporate loyalty,* and its expectations of executive—and management—level personnel must be made clear through its executive and management development programs. Its effectiveness in transmitting a proper balance between corporate loyalty and personal conscience will, in large measure, determine its corporate image and its appearance to the society as a whole.

The factors typically considered desirable in a corporate image, as judged by advertising, internal communication programs and executive utterances, are:

1. The corporation, through its products and services, contributes to the public good.
2. The corporation is engaged in exciting and vital scientific and technological research.
3. The corporation maintains a benevolent—almost paternalistic —policy toward its personnel.
4. The corporation is committed to supporting and encouraging the best in the surrounding cultural milieu.

The strength and nature of the corporate image will be determined by the organization's ability to transmit these values to its leadership personnel. For just as school children reflect their home and school environments, so does the adult reflect the environment of his world of work.

The Company and the Community

It is the company's relationship to the community as a whole that helps to shape its educational policies and activities. It has been shown that the desire to solidify that relationship and render it mutually beneficial underlies the planning of the executive and management development program. Technical training programs offered by private industry are helping to upgrade the work force of the community and the nation.

Another important dimension in the relationship between the company and the community involves corporate support of public

TABLE III

TYPES OF ASSISTANCE

Grants for current operations:		
Unrestricted	$16,561,436	24.0%
Fellowships and Scholarships	11,700,190	17.0%
Indirect grants	6,879,435	10.0%
Matching grants	3,512,965	5.1%
Basic research	3,421,430	4.9%
Departmental grants	3,152,500	4.6%
Cost-of-education supplements	1,498,976	2.2%
Faculty compensation	1,007,417	1.5%
Other purposes	6,041,928	8.7%
	$53,776,277	78.0%
Grants for capital purposes:		
Capital uses, open	$ 8,669,606	12.5%
Buildings and equipment	6,325,582	9.2%
Endowment	210,375	0.3%
	$15,205,563	22.0%

Source: Aid-To-Education Programs of Some Leading Business Concerns (New York: Council for Financial Aid to Education, Inc., 1962), p. 6.

educational activities, which has been steadily increasing since the end of World War II. A survey of corporate support to education in 1962, conducted by the Council for Financial Aid to Education, Inc., revealed that 610 companies had contributed a total of $68,981,840. The specific purposes for which the various sums were contributed are shown in Table III.

There are several statements which can be made with respect to the general subject of corporate support of education, which are supported by present-day corporate-fund practices as well as legal opinions. Generally corporations have a recognized responsibility, a correlative right, and potential advantage in contributing within reasonable limits to charitable and educational institutions. The principal reasons for the expenditure of corporate funds in support of education are:

1. Favorable environment. In the A. P. Smith case in New Jersey in 1953, a landmark in the field of corporate philanthrophy, the court declared that

> corporate boards may contribute for purposes which, in their judgment . . . will conduce to the betterment of social and economic conditions, thereby permitting such corporations, as creatures af this state, to discharge their obligations to society while, at the same time, reaping the benefits which essentially accrue to them through public recognition of their existence within the economic and social, as well as within the legal, structure of society.

2. Development of people. It is generally recognized by commentators on the current scene that education is assuming the role of the key parameter in the treatment of many of our social and economic problems.

Education is both the root of technological change and the basis for successful adaptation to the problems it presents. We must become a more versatile people, with more skills and broader understanding of our place in a fast-changing world. The key to progress was well described by The American Assembly report[20] devoted to technology and education as "a new national attitude, in which education is universally welcomed. A vast expansion in our facilities for scientific, technical, and professional education will, of course, be a necessary part of our preparation for speedier technological change."

3. Mutuality of interest in knowledge and research. Since

---

[20] John T. Dunlop, ed., *Automation and Technological Change* (Englewood Cliffs, N.J.: Prentice-Hall, Inc., 1962).

the middle 1930's the national research and development budget has increased sharply, yet the percentage of such research done in the university community is declining. A persuasive case for the support of basic research in education can be made, as in the *President's Science Advisory Committee Report (1960)*[21] which states that "teaching and basic research must go hand in hand." Undoubtedly organizations such as IBM, AT&T, and General Motors and the Federal Government are pushing applied science. However, the nourishment of such research by basic exploration in the university community is lagging behind. The report cited indicates the necessity of doubling our first-rate institutions from the approximately 15–20 that exist today. Excellence must be promoted at all levels. Corporate aid to education should effectively involve the interchange of scientific and professional talent as well as the support of truly basic research.

4. Strengthening the pluralistic education system. a) Basic to maintaining and expanding our national leadership in a competitive world is the keystone: education; at all levels, public and private. American education must continue to be characterized by variety of content and dispersion of control and support. b) Support should not be determined completely by the issue of privately vs. publicly supported institutions. American education at the higher level must maintain a healthy balance, though changing, and not tied to given percentages, between public and private support. As a major factor in our economy's private sector, industry is a prime and growing source of financial support to education. The leverage of private funds in offsetting state control is immeasurable. By any default on industry's part in supporting education, there is pressure upon government to make it up, perhaps leading to an unhealthy alteration of traditional private-public balance. Both state supported and private institutions need help from *all* private sectors of the economy.

> The trend of recent years has been toward a growing reliance on public institutions and a growing dependence of both public and private institutions on public funds. With respect to total income the support of endowment and gifts has fallen from 20% to 16%. Over-all, the support of government has risen from 36% to 50% ... A most significant recent development has been the increasing

---

[21] *Scientific Progress, the Universities and the Federal Government.* Report of the President's Science Advisory Committee (Washington, D.C.: USGPO November 1960.)

dependence of private institutions on public funds . . . 1956 private institutions derived 21% of their income from government as compared to less than 2% in 1930.[22]

5. Public relations dividends. Beyond fulfillment of "corporate citizenship" responsibilities there is significant potential for public relations return on the education support investment. Recognition of this by some leading companies (e.g., Ford and GE) followed fast upon the widening of managerial discretion in corporate giving that resulted from the affirmative Smith Case decision.

Certain companies not only have mounted enlightened programs of support but appropriately are communicating them to the education community, stockholders, employees, and the public in general.

In summary, these five are the basic factors behind corporate support of education. Our legal environment encourages it, as noted in the Smith Case decision. And furthermore, our corporate tax structure, providing up to 5% of net profit engaged in such efforts, tax free, is intended to promote it.

---

[22] *Financing Higher Education 1960–70* (New York: McGraw-Hill Book Company, Inc., 1959).

CHAPTER IV

Educational and Training Programs
for the Individual

The most commonly accepted educational activity in business is the training program for the individual worker. These programs fall into one of several general categories: manufacturing education, engineering and research, service training, marketing training, customer training, and company-wide programs of various kinds.

Manufacturing Training Program

Apprenticeship programs. The history of the apprenticeship system, its practice in the Middle Ages, and its development since then have already been discussed (see pp. 2–3). The present-day apprenticeship program is somewhat different: it combines classroom instruction and on-the-job practice. An agreement signed by apprentice and employer (and generally subject to supervision by joint apprenticeship committees) specifies the length of service. The usual term of service is 8,000 hours, or four years, at the beginning of which the apprentice is paid the minimum wage established for that particular craft or trade. As the apprentice moves toward completion of his training, his wages are gradually raised.

Today, companies such as General Motors and IBM take great pride in their apprenticeship programs. A recent General Motors ad[1] pointed out that, within the company, 2700 apprentices are being trained in a total of thirty trades, among which are pipe fitting, bricklaying, and die sinking. Because the programs are formalized and subject to review by joint apprenticeship committees, the apprentices are assured of good wages on a rising scale, and standardized training procedures. At the conclusion of the four-year course, the apprentices have acquired skills which will serve them in good stead throughout their working careers. They are also free to work anywhere they wish, although of course most of them choose to remain with the company in order to retain the fringe

---

[1] *The Saturday Review* (August 1964).

benefits they have accumulated during their four years of service.

The medieval requirement of a masterpiece before an apprentice could be admitted into the ranks of the master craftsmen has fallen into disuse. Nevertheless, one areawide apprenticeship program in Chicago, designed to transmit the skills of pattern making for use in the production of castings, requires apprentices (as part of the final examination) to execute, without supervision, a contract job ordered by a customer or a pattern making shop. The quality of the work performance is judged by the area joint labor-management apprenticeship committee which awards the final certificate. It must be stressed, however, that this is the exception rather than the rule.

The administration of apprenticeship programs within a given company generally falls within the area of responsibility of the co-ordinator or director of training and education in the manufacturing or production functions. Such individuals have usually been through such apprenticeship programs themselves and are therefore appreciative of the benefits involved and knowledgeable about the problems encountered.

Despite the success of the modern apprenticeship program, the number of graduates of such programs lags far behind the actual needs of industry. One reason for this is the attrition rate caused by the promotion of graduate apprentices to managerial or super-visory positions. Because production and manufacturing processes are scheduled on the basis of economic considerations, the demands for apprenticeship programs vary. This variation makes it difficult to plan long-range programs to offset the inevitable attrition rate.

Another reason for the lag behind industrial needs is that the contract and indenture period traditionally associated with the ap-prenticeship system is not widely accepted by American youth. Finally, the apprenticeship programs for certain crafts or industries are rigidly controlled by the labor union involved, and acceptance into these programs, unless one is related to or sponsored by a union member, may be difficult or impossible.

Clearly, the size and scope of the apprenticeship program must be stepped up if the ever-growing needs of the economy for skilled labor are to be met. Another reason for enlarging the industrial apprenticeship program is that many of the tools, instruments, and materials required to train workers in modern trade techniques often lie beyond the financial capabilities of the public school system or private technical institute. And only in the industrial program does the apprentice have the incalculable advantage of working alongside skilled craftsmen using the latest and most effective techniques.

The benefits of the industrial apprenticeship program for the individual who completes his training were outlined in the report of a study recently made by the U.S. Department of Labor:

> Six years after completing the program
> * More than one-fourth had advanced to supervisory positions or had become managers or proprietors of businesses.
> * 93 per cent had made specific use of the skills learned during their apprenticeships.[5]

Unfortunately, the number of registered apprentices in the United States is declining; it has already fallen from a peak of 225,000 in 1950 to 132,000 in 1960–61. (See Table IV.)

TABLE IV

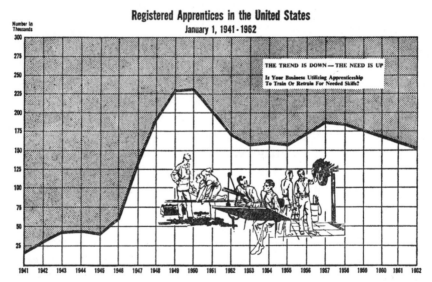

Registered Apprentices in the United States
January 1, 1941 - 1962

THE TREND IS DOWN — THE NEED IS UP
Is Your Business Utilizing Apprenticeship To Train Or Retrain For Needed Skills?

Source: "Apprenticeship: An Answer to Training Needs of Business," U.S. Chamber of Commerce *Special Supplement* (Washington, D.C.: February 8, 1963).

There are now approximately 8.5 million skilled workers in industry; it is estimated that some 25 per cent more will be needed by 1970.[6] These figures, together with the constant and increasing

---

[5] "Apprenticeship: An Answer to Training Needs of Business," U.S. Chamber of Commerce *Special Supplement* (Washington, D.C.: February 8, 1963).

[6] "Apprenticeship: An Answer to Training Needs of Business," U.S. Chamber of Commerce *Special Supplement* (Washington, D.C.: February 8, 1963).

loss of skilled workers who move into higher-level positions, pose a critical problem in the American economy. One of the solutions to this problem can and must involve the combination of the resources of private industry and those of the state and federal governments, and the devotion of these resources to the expansion and improvement of industrial apprenticeship programs.

On-the-job training program. A substantial part of the training activities in business and industry consists of on-the-job training, which differs from apprenticeship training in several important respects. For example, the typical apprenticeship program involves a formal contract between apprentice and employer, a fixed term of service, and is generally designed to transmit a craftlike skill or set of skills. On-the-job training, on the other hand, involves no formal contract and the length of the training program varies according to the skills to be taught. It is, essentially, a learning-by-doing method. Most important, the on-the-job training program is generally devoted to teaching the individual a work process—a set of skills determined by the current technology of a particular aspect of production. Thus the skills acquired through an on-the-job training program are typically less immediately transferable than those possessed by a graduate apprentice. Nevertheless, on-the-job training compares favorably with apprenticeship program in the amount of material taught.

On-the-job training, in practice, has two basic functions: 1. To introduce new workers to the work process by allowing them to learn through observations and productive contribution; 2. To upgrade and retrain workers whose old skills cannot meet the requirements of changes in the technical or manufacturing process. The trainee is given some classroom instruction as well as work experience, and is paid at a rate commensurate with his experience and seniority. On-the-job training programs, unlike apprenticeship programs, are usually carried on under the direction of the work superviser, with occasional help from the coordinator of training and education within the manufacturing or production function.

Because of the informal nature of the on-the-job training program, accurate figures on the total cost and the number of personnel involved are hard to come by. It is not unreasonable to estimate that some 3–5 per cent of the work force in a typical manufacturing operation is undergoing some type of on-the-job training at any one time. When we consider the size of the work force, it is clear that the total, though largely unseen, cost runs into the hundreds of millions of dollars each year. The number of personnel involved is even more difficult to estimate. Because the process consists chiefly of learning by doing, many companies have not formalized their on-the-job training programs. Those that have reported a total of 2.5 million trainees in 1962. The range of industries involved, and the distribution of trainees among them is indicated in Table V.

TABLE V

DISTRIBUTION OF TRAINEES IN FORMAL TRAINING
BY INDUSTRY

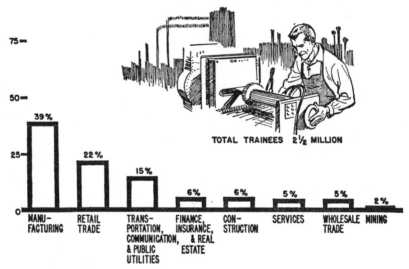

Source: "On-the-Job Training: An Answer to Training Needs of Business," U.S. Chamber of Commerce *Special Supplement* (Washington, D.C.: June 28, 1963).

The responsibilities of the coordinator of the programs are manifold. He must make certain that appropriate numbers of trainees are introduced into the program, that the teaching techniques employed are effective to the task involved, and that the program itself reflects the requirements posed by the latest changes in technical production processes. He must also determine appropriate course content and length of instruction period, and he must devise adequate methods of testing and measurement. Finally, since most large organizations have abandoned haphazard methods of introducing individuals to the work process, the training supervisor is increasingly finding himself called upon to assist in individual counselling and career determination.

The growing importance of the on-the-job training program is emphasized in its relationship to the problem of vocational education:

> An appropriate division of labor is called for between education and industry, with education doing what it can do best (educate more broadly for a life of work and citizenship), and industry doing what it can do best (train for the specific job). Such a relationship already exists in engineering: educators in the various disciplines have paid considerable attention to the improvement of the liberal and related knowledge content of the engineering curriculum, . . . industry has accepted the necessity of spending a longer time breaking in the recent graduate . . .
> On the other hand, the industrial complex of the nation is being made and remade so swiftly, and plant and worker mobility are so high that narrow, local training may have short relevance for the new worker. This again points to the importance of a more broadly based vocational-technical education, one consonant with long-term regional and national manpower demands.[7]

New devices and new procedures are being sought to bring together the capabilities and resources of industry and the administrative structure and capacities of the vocational education apparatus. The Smith-Hughes Act and the George-Barden Act limit vocational instruction for employed workers to that which is designed to update or upgrade his knowledge or skill in his present occupational field. No provision is made for the unemployed worker who must develop new skills, or for the employed worker who seeks training in a new occupation.

This need is partly filled by the Manpower Development and Training Act, which established a nationwide program for both institutional and on-the-job training programs to meet current and future occupational demands. The U.S. Department of Labor's Bureau of Apprenticeship and Training, which is responsible for implementing this provision of the Act, assists employers and schools in setting up appropriate training programs and, in some cases, helps to defray the costs incurred (for trainer salaries, supplies, and the like). The Act gives the Secretary of Labor a broad mandate to develop such programs and to secure their adoption— not only by employers, but also by state, public, and private agencies; trade associations; labor organizations; and other qualified industrial and community groups. For the more formal on-the-job training programs, which supplement training with classroom work,

---

[7] Venn, *op. cit.*, p. 33.

appropriate arrangements for instruction are made through the Department of Health, Education, and Welfare.

Thus the Act embodies a striking new concept—one involving the cooperation of private industry, labor organizations, government agencies, and the schools in a concerted, united effort to solve a problem of national concern. This approach also adds a new dimension to the responsibility of the coordinator or supervisor of the training program: he must seek not only to satisfy the requirements of his own company, but also to contribute his insights and knowledge to those of others who are engaged in the wider and more far-reaching aspects of the task at hand. The successful coordination of these efforts and the extension of this cooperative program can have profound implications for the future of training and education, both in business and in the schools.

Work-study programs.   Work-study programs are designed to alternate work assignments in business and industry with class attendance at high school or college. The early pioneers in the 1900's included the University of Cincinnati and Northeastern University, who introduced programs of cooperative education in which the student might apply to practical work situations the knowledge and theory gained in school. Although originally identified with engineering education, the work-study program now embraces the liberal arts, vocational education, and business administration.

On the college level, most work-study programs are organized on the "two-man team" principle, which involves the pairing off of students participating in the program. A full-time job, in a private concern or governmental agency, is shared by each pair of students; one member of the "team" works while the other attends school. Then, at the midterm or after a certain period of time, the two change places. The advantages of the team system are that it permits a given job to be continuously filled while assuring that educational facilities are not left unutilized.

> Because cooperative education is commonly organized so that half the student body is at work while the other half is on the campus, the plan permits more efficient utilization of the college plant and other facilities. Many colleges use their facilities little, if at all, during the summer. In most cooperative programs, the plant is used throughout the year. This arrangement also makes it possible to graduate more students than the conventional programs using the same facilities. From 14 per cent to 60 per cent more students can be graduated, the exact percentage depending upon the rotation

plan, the number of years during the student's career when he is involved in a work-study plan, and the number of years the program has been in operation.[8]

At a time when the constant rise in college enrollments is expected to accelerate still further, the possibility of deriving maximum utility from existing facilities cannot be dismissed as a negligible consideration.

The college-level work-study program is normally under the supervision of the coordinator of education and training in the engineering and/or manufacturing functions. He works together with representatives of the various colleges to make sure that each student is given the most effective combination of work experience and formal courses. This is important, for if the work-study program is to serve its purpose, each student must be given a work assignment which will complement and utilize his educational background and provide applicable experience for his future career.

Carefully planned and executed, the college-level work-study program carries benefits, not only for the student, but also for the participating college and business concern and the community as a whole.

For example, the coordination of a relevant work experience with the school's educational program increases student motivation in his formal studies. As the student comes to see the practical applicability of knowledge gained in the classroom, his interest in and respect for academic work begins to rise. Meanwhile, the work experience helps him to develop a sense of responsibility for his own efforts and requires him to exercise his judgment in matters involving decisions, thus raising his level of maturity and preparing him for the challenges and responsibilities of the adult world.

These benefits to the student are, through him, transmitted to the college. The student's contact with the attitudes, values, and requirements of the outside world helps to bring a new dimension to the classroom, breaking down the isolation of the inner-oriented academic community. This, together with the more tangible benefits discussed earlier, makes it clear that it is to the advantage of the colleges to participate in these work-study programs.

The benefits of the work-study programs for business and the community are equally clear. The growing demands of the econ-

---

[8] E. H. Lyons and James W. Wilson, *Work-Study College Programs* (New York: Harper & Row, 1961), p. 7.

omy, estimated for future decades, require that more and more trained workers at all levels be added to the labor force each year. Work-study programs make it possible for employers to select potentially capable people and to train them over a period of time, thus observing them and evaluating their performance before making a firm commitment to their employment. This preview, as it were, of the worker before he actually joins the labor force reduces the expenses and uncertainties of recruitment—expenses which are customarily borne directly by the employers and indirectly by the community as a whole.

In 1963, some 30,000 students participated in work-study programs in more than sixty colleges, junior colleges, technical institutes, and graduate schools.[9] The National Commission for Cooperative Education, formed by educators and industrial leaders to widen the scope of the work-study concept, has as its goal the raising of the number of participating collegiate institutions and students to 125 and 75,000, respectively, by 1970. The Commission also hopes to encourage the adoption of the work-study pattern in new professional and technical fields. The importance of this goal was indicated in a statement by the National Industrial Conference Board:

> Perhaps the most rapidly expanding field is that of technical occupations, especially in industry. Estimates of needs for technicians at the present ratio of 0.7 to 1 of engineers to scientists indicate some 70,000 new technicians required annually. If the ratio of technicians to engineers is increased to 2 to 1, as many feel is necessary, the need jumps to 200,000 persons per year.[10]

The need for programs of cooperative education is no less great on the high school level. Indeed, the need may be even more pressing at this level, for the work-study program has been shown to be effective both in combatting the appalling dropout rate in the nation's high schools and in upgrading and updating the vocational education offered there.

There are four major types of vocational education cooperative programs:

1. Industrial Cooperative Training
2. Diversified Occupations Training

---

9 *National Commission for Cooperative Education Report.*
10 *Employee Education.* Studies in Personnel Policy No. 119 (New York: National Industrial Conference Board, 1951).

3. Cooperative Office Occupations Training
4. Cooperative Retailing Occupations Training [11]

These programs are designed to provide high school students, sixteen years of age and over, with an opportunity to acquire marketable skills in an occupation for which they have an aptitude. Student aptitudes are determined through a process of testing, individual counseling, and review of school records and demonstrated interests. It is important that the student be suited to the particular program and vice versa, because one of the major aims of the program is the student's future employment in that industry, preferably by the same employer.

The benefits of the high school work-study program are similar to those on the college level. The increased academic motivation of the student, which so often results from participation in a relevant and satisfying work experience, is particularly important in the high schools, for the lack of such motivation is a major contributing factor in the rising dropout rates of the past few years. Because he usually has no work experience and no marketable skills, and because the number of jobs open to unskilled workers is rapidly decreasing, the dropout is becoming a growing burden to himself, to the economy, and to the community. Current programs designed to train students who have dropped out of school must cope with the problem (in many cases) of already fixed patterns of joblessness, poverty, and discouragement. They also represent an added expense for those who finance the programs—whether these be private concerns, or the public (through state and federal governments). These are costs and problems which might well be avoided by an effective work-study program, and it is to the advantage of business concerns, government agencies, and education officials to cooperate in developing and expanding such programs. In 1962, more than 20,000 students were enrolled in the Cooperative Industrial Training Program, and some 44,000 were participating in the Cooperative Retailing Occupation Training Program.[12] Nevertheless, such programs have only begun to make a dent in the dropout problem; if they are to provide an effective solution, they

---

[11] "Work-Study Programs: An Answer to Training Needs of Business." U.S. Chamber of Commerce *Special Supplement* (Washington, D.C.: October 11, 1963). The specific occupations within these categories should require a minimum of 2,000 hours training before proficiency is reached.

[12] *Ibid.*

must be greatly multiplied and expanded over the next five to ten years.

Engineering and Research Training Programs

The constantly accelerating rate of scientific and technological progress makes it essential that every company whose products or services are based upon such processes establish and maintain a continuing program of education and training designed to upgrade and update the skills of its engineers and technicians. The rapidity with which scientific and technological innovations are introduced into the modern production process has created an ever-widening gap between the engineering theories taught in the colleges and technical institutes and the engineering practices found on the production line. Cooperative efforts by engineering school faculties and practicing engineers are doing much to bridge this gap; nevertheless, the young graduate engineer who joins an industrial firm must undergo a period of orientation—not only to the company, but also to the technological innovations introduced since the publication of his latest textbook.

Another dimension to engineering education is posed by the fact that the educational "half-life" of the engineer is less than a decade. This means that the engineer is faced with the problem of upgrading a major portion of his knowledge at least every ten years. And because the new knowledge is usually based on higher mathematical and scientific skills, its acquisition may require that the engineer attend full-time courses at some institute of higher education. Therefore, the company's own program of engineering education must be designed to include provisions for on-campus courses lasting a full semester or longer.

Finally, the growing importance of technical processes in industrial operations is casting a corresponding emphasis on the role of the engineer in the company. More and more engineers and scientists are rising to positions of managerial and executive authority. The company that promotes them has a responsibility for making sure that their managerial talents—particularly as these are applied to technical and engineering operations—are exploited and developed.

Thus the various needs of modern industry have given rise to a broad program of engineering education. It includes, in addition to courses offered by the company's own program of engineering training and education, degree and nondegree on-campus courses, engineering management programs, and professional society meetings.

Nondegree on-site courses. One procedure for updating and refreshing the technical skills and knowledge of engineers is the nondegree on-site course. Such courses are usually given in the company's own laboratories and are generally supervised by the training director of the laboratory concerned with a set of specific engineering functions. Instructors are drawn from company personnel and, occasionally, the staffs of nearby universities.

Classes meet during and after working hours. Some companies offer "early-bird" courses, with classes meeting before the start of the working day. Class periods run from one to two hours, and are usually planned on the basis of five per week. Still other companies offer such courses as part of a Saturday morning education program. A given course may run from one week to three months, depending on its purpose and on the scope of the material covered.

On-site degree courses. The growing need for the expansion and updating of knowledge by scientists and engineers has given rise to cooperative efforts between industrial engineering laboratories and nearby universities. The goal of these efforts is to provide an opportunity for scientists and engineers to pursue, on a part-time basis, programs leading to the master's or doctoral degrees. Such programs would include courses on higher mathematics, wave theory, engineering economics, and other graduate-level subjects.

Admission requirements for these courses are the same as those which govern admission to university courses. Students are selected on the basis of their educational background and their academic performance. Minimum grade averages must be maintained for admission to specific courses and for continuation in the program.

In one typical program, classes meet in the company laboratories two days a week during working hours. The instructors commute from the university campus. All the expenses involved—for materials and for instruction—are borne by the company.

Graduate-level on-site programs carry vast advantages both for the participants and for the sponsoring companies. The student benefits by being introduced to theory within the work environment; thus he is able to see clearly the application of theory to his own work. The company benefits because the research projects undertaken in class usually involve company problems; thus the company is often able to put to profitable use the results obtained in class.

A major problem in developing an effective graduate-level on-site program is the engagement of the best possible instructors. In this matter, of course, the company located in the vicinity of universities with outstanding engineering faculties enjoys a distinct advantage. There is also the danger that the student will come to view the engineering or scientific discipline in terms of his company's problems and goals, ignoring the wider applications with which he might come into contact as an on-campus student. The problem of "inbred" training may be largely offset by providing an opportunity for these students to attend occasional summer sessions at the university.

Indeed, some companies prefer to encourage their engineers and scientists to pursue all their graduate-level studies on university campuses. The on-campus program, designed specifically to upgrade engineering skills in particular areas, include a tremendous range of short summer courses. Some of the on-campus programs are designed to develop engineering management skills, and follow the general form of the graduate business school company training program. Several major technical institutes offer a one-year on-campus program for intensive depth study of a given engineering discipline, or for general studies in engineering management.

Resident university programs. Some companies offer programs designed to allow outstanding professional employees to pursue courses leading to advanced degrees on university campuses. The advantage of such a program is that it allows the student to obtain his degree in a much shorter period of time than would be true if he were confined to on-site courses. One company considers employees participating in on-campus degree programs to be on work assignments. Not only are the employees' tuition fees and other school charges paid in full, but they also receive during their period of study full salary and all the benefits accruing from the company's personnel policies.

The on-campus program varies in length, depending on the degree sought. Usually, one year is required for the master's degree, and three years for the doctorate. Doctoral assignments, however, are subject to annual review; the assignment is renewed only if warranted by the student's academic performance during the previous year.

Participants in on-campus graduate programs are selected on the basis of their performance on competitive examinations, the evaluation of their potential contribution to the company, and their acceptance by the graduate school involved. These rigorous selective procedures are justified when one considers the expense involved in such a program; management must assure that those employees are selected who are most likely to do well in graduate-level work. Usually great pains are taken to avoid the impression that participation in the program is a "reward" for good performance on the job.

Reactions to this type of program have been varied. One company that had offered such a program for several years has now revised its provisions to include only partial support for full-time study. The principal reason for this retrenchment is the fact that the career placement of employees with doctoral degrees is not assured as a result of their study. The company decided that the funds allotted for the support of education would be more effectively used if distributed over a more broadly based program which allowed wider participation.

Part-time on-campus degree programs.   More and more companies offer degree programs which are designed to include both on-site and on-campus study. Such schools as Stanford University, the University of Kentucky, and New York University participate in these programs. Usually the engineers work in the company laboratory in the morning and attend classes at the university in the afternoon. The actual time allowed for on-campus study varies with the type of program and with the company. One company allows up to eight hours a week for courses leading to a master's degree, and twelve hours a week for courses leading to a doctorate. The Polytechnic Institute of Brooklyn participates in a program in which the engineers take on-site part-time courses during the academic year, and then attend short, intensive courses at the Institute during the summer. In this case, the Institute grants academic credit for the on-site courses and permits research projects on company problems to be presented as partial fulfillment of degree requirements. One company selected approximately 250 employees with bachelor's degrees in science, engineering, or mathematics for participation in a special two-year program. The participants pursued courses in basic mathematics, engineering, and computer programming during the first summer, then elementary and advanced courses during the rest of the year. Their weekly schedules involved one full day of formal instruction and four days of on-the-job training. At the end of the first year, half the group was assigned to the second phase of the program. In the second year, the weekly schedules of participants involve two days of formal instruction at the nearby technical institute and three days of on-the-job training. Those who successfully complete both phases of the two-year program are awarded a Master of Science degree.

Part-time on-campus degree programs naturally require a high degree of cordination between the business concern and the institute involved. But the results are well worth the effort: the combination of formal instruction at the university and work experience at the company laboratory helps the participating engineer to see the application of theory to his own work problems and to the general field of his specialty.

Engineering management programs. Engineering management programs are designed to upgrade and refresh the professional skills of those employees responsible for the high-level management of technical functions. One such program, cooperatively developed by the University of California and General Electric, covers various fields of modern science as they relate to current engineering practice. Its goal is to bring engineering executives up-to-date on those scientific and technological advances which have been made since the end of their own formal training in the field. It also attempts to provide an insight into the basic concepts of the different disciplines and an understanding of the communication and control procedures needed to coordinate and manage the various specialties. Some of the formal courses offered cover such topics as:

Classical mathematics	Probabilistic Mathematics
Atomic theory and nucleonics	Solid state physics
Relativity	Tensor analysis
Electromagnetic theory	Metallurgy and fracture
Nuclear power	Transport phenomena
Energy Conversion—Fuel cells	Chemistry
Cybernetics of living systems	Stress and vibration analysis
Statistical mechanics and wave mechanics	
Control, Communications, and Computers	

The need for such programs is pressing. Because of the rapidity of technological change, the modern engineering executive often finds himself charged with the responsibility for evaluating and managing projects and phenomena, the complexity of which are far beyond the scope of his own now-distant formal education. He is expected to guide and to judge the efforts of subordinates trained in such fields as plasmic physics, cryogenics, and dynamic programming—concepts still unknown when the textbooks from which he studied were written. If he is to fulfill his responsibility satisfactorily, the engineering executive must be allowed an opportunity to bring himself up-to-date on the advances made in his own specialty and in related fields.

Professional society activities. Besides sponsoring their own program of education, many companies encourage employee participation in programs of technical education sponsored by local engineering societies and other professional associations. The engineering society in Cleveland, for instance, offers a program which includes courses in management planning and control, computers, value analysis, patent protection, economics, construction engineering, and operations research. Classes meet one evening a week for ten weeks. The teaching staff is composed of practicing engineers from local divisions of industrial concerns, and members of the faculties of nearby universities and technical institutes.

And there is the American Management Association, one of the principal organizations concerned with better management, which sponsors a number of educational activities, among which are seminars, conferences, and periodicals. The four membership periodicals are *Personnel,* which deals not only with management-labor problems but with the whole spectrum of human relations; *Management News,* an illustrated summary of the Association's activities and their relation to current management problems: *The Management Review,* a summary of significant articles from important business publications; and *The Manager's Letter,* which offers concise information on new management ideas and trends. The Association also publishes books, research studies, reports, and bulletins dealing with significant management problems.

The seminars include the Workshop Seminar, in which experienced operating executives from different companies compare problems and exchange information on successful systems and methods; the Orientation Seminar, in which both new and experienced executives are given a brief review of fundamental management principles and brought up-to-date on the latest developments in the field; and the VTR Seminar, in which speakers—all executives of vast experience—are presented on video-tape recordings.

Marketing Education Programs

The complexities of society, the growth in consumer demands, and the increased number of products and services have cast a new emphasis on the role of marketing in the over-all business operation. Not only must the market be informed of and persuaded to accept company policies, products, and services, but its opinions and desires must be discerned and considered by the company in order that it may continue to function in a profitable manner. The marketing function, as it is described in most large companies, embraces the administration and planning of the marketplace, the introduction and sale of new products, the sales engineering required to match the resources of the company and its market, and the engineering and administrative service to be offered the customer.

Marketing problems. Typical marketing problems are intimately connected with problems of education and training. Because success within a free economy is based on increased distribution and the stimulation of new markets, a company's well-being—both financial and organizational—is a function of the performance of its sales staff. The traditional concept of the hard sell is fast disappearing from the business scene. Today's salesman must reflect the image his company strives so hard to create. He must not only stimulate new demand and encourage the acceptance of new ideas, he must also be a responsible agent in providing advice and information on changes in product technology and services.

The maintenance of an effective sales force depends upon a program of technical upgrading. Companies devote much money and effort to the development of sales engineering teams, which provide a direct link between the engineering functions and the sales situation. The successful sales engineer must have training in product and service technologies in addition to training in sales skills. Therefore a sales engineering program must include a host of courses in both general and technical fields.

The final element in the marketing function is the provision of administrative or engineering service. Service engineers must be trained to provide service for equipment delivered, maintenance service for equipment installed, and consulting service for operational problems. They must also be trained to provide administrative service: information on company procedures and policies.

Thus the three elements of the marketing function—sales, sales engineering, and service engineering—are based upon a program of intensive and extensive training. The length of training and the specific course content vary according to the company involved. The following discussion will examine in detail the activities of one large concern, engaged in selling equipment in the capital goods market to other industrial concerns. Its program is typical, in organization and goal, of those sponsored by other large organizations.

Sales training. Sales trainees are hired by local branch offices, usually as the result of recruiting programs sponsored at local colleges and universities. Very rarely is a non-college graduate accepted; many sales trainees have master's degrees in business administration or engineering. Applicants must display native intelligence, a wide range of interests, and a potential ability to work well with people.

Sales trainees report for a one-week orientation program in the branch office. (Occasionally the program may include employees from other departments who have been selected for opportunities in the sales division.) Trainees spend one day with the service engineering group, two days with an operating salesman, one day with the administrative staff, and one day with the branch manager. Then they are given six individual self-study courses outlining the nature of the company products, its uses and applications, and a history of the company and its policies.

As soon as possible after the first week, the trainees are sent to one of the company's district education centers. The eight-week program there includes an introduction to the fundamentals of record-keeping, a survey of the operating principles of the company's chief products, and an intensive study of business procedures. The trainees watch technical demonstrations of the equipment and films showing it in actual use. They are given practice problems, the solutions to which are tested on the machines. Finally, they take part in simulated sales calls in which they learn the essentials of the sales operation.

At the end of the period, the trainee returns to the branch office for on-the-job experience with these machines. He also takes part in an eight-week program designed to familiarize him with all aspects of field sales activities, including customer operations, equipment installation, and selling procedures. The trainee, working directly with a senior salesman, plans and works through a sales situation, participates in sales meetings, and prepares material in extension courses offered by the central sales training office.

At the end of the job apprenticeship period, the trainee returns to the district education center for a three-week course in the principles of the company's more advanced equipment. A major feature of the program is a comprehensive case study designed to give him practice in all aspects of installation, including systems selection, the development of appropriate techniques and procedures, and so on. Then he returns to the branch office for practical experience in the installation of this advanced equipment.

The final phase of the program begins with a five-week course at one of the company's two major education centers. There the trainee studies in detail the application of all company equipment to a wide range of uses. He is then assigned to a branch office for twenty-four weeks. There, under the supervision of a senior salesman and the branch manager, he gains experience in the installation of new systems and the extension of the use of already installed equipment. He continues to make sales calls (with the senior salesman), participates in sales training meetings, and undertakes more extension courses.

At the conclusion of this training period certain trainees are sent to a central sales and marketing training school to specialize in the operations of a major industry and the use of the company's equipment in segments of that industry. The five-week course consists of lectures, seminars, practice calls, demonstrations, and criticisms. Guest lecturers from the industry or from nearby universities explain specific industry applications or policy areas. As a final exercise, the trainees must prepare and present team proposals for a specific industrial application. If this test of the trainee's two-year study of theory and practice in the specialized and professional application of the company's products is satisfactory, he is ready to join a team handling a group of large accounts in his particular industry.

Those trainees who are to be given general sales territories are trained to handle smaller accounts and to develop new business. After a generalized program at the company's sales training school and some field experience, these trainees may also be given depth training in a specific industry.

This comprehensive sales training program produces salesmen who can work directly with the product, understand its many applications, and deal effectively with all levels of management in the customer organization.

Sales engineering. Sales engineers also receive product and applications training. Instead of going on to sales training, however, they receive extensive experience in all phases of problem definition and the organization and system design leading to installation. They are trained in the preparation of proposals, the training of customers, and the preparation of technical material used in systems analysis. They also serve a one-year branch office apprenticeship, during which they undertake formal depth study of specific products and systems.

Then they attend a five-week program at one of the company's two major education centers. There they probe in depth the new applications, receive practical machine experience, and simulate actual situations in a customer's operations. Practice problems including the planting of deliberate "bugs" in order to develop the students' diagnostic techniques.

Sales engineering trainees are then assigned to a very large company-operated installation for experience in the use of equipment for such advanced applications as problem-solving in areas of advanced forecasting, scientific computation, and the like. The final examination includes the development of a full-scale project demonstrating their knowledge and command of systems analysis. Qualified sales engineers are then assigned to branch offices, but they continue to receive periodic retraining on new equipment, new techniques, and new applications.

The top one or two per cent of the sales engineering force is sent to the company's graduate-level facility, which is devoted to developing and teaching new methods in the design and use of company equipment. The sales engineers attend lectures and research seminars and participate in team projects. The school term lasts twelve weeks, but the number of courses and class hours varies with the individual. At the conclusion of the twelve-week course, the sales engineer has a complete command of the company's products and services in a specific area of application.

Service engineering.   Service engineering trainees are hired by the local branch manager and service manager. They are usually recent graduates of colleges or technical school, although employees from other departments may occasionally be selected for training in this function.

The new trainees are given remedial training (if necessary) in such subjects as physics and mathematics. They attend formal classes and extension courses offered by the service engineering department.

After this orientation period, the trainee spends ten to fourteen weeks at one of the company's three education centers devoted to field service engineering, where they study and practice the maintenance and repair of the smaller equipment in the company's product line. Then they return to the branch office where, under the direction of senior service engineers, they gain experience in the servicing of this equipment.

Those trainees who display appropriate aptitude and interest are sent back to the education center to study the servicing of advanced equipment. Courses may last from several days to eight weeks, depending on the complexity of the equipment studied. The equipment is "bugged" by instructors so that the trainees may learn to trace and diagnose malfunctions. These laboratory sessions are supplemented by lectures and audio-visual demonstrations of the fundamentals and advanced uses of the equipment.

The branch offices maintain a continuing program of field training under the direction of product experts. Those service engineers who have received advanced training will, in turn, help to prepare other service engineers in the use of new equipment. Field training programs last from one day to three months, depending on the complexity of the equipment being studied.

Because service engineers are also responsible for promoting and maintaining good company-customer relationships, they also receive a good deal of formal and informal training in the appropriate methods of dealing with the customer's nontechnical problems as well.

It can be seen that this company's marketing education program is designed to provide maximum service and satisfaction for its customers. The program, which is under the general direction of the director of marketing education, also benefits the company, for it provides a system of feedback whereby product deficiencies, customer attitudes and needs, and other important information is transmitted to those responsible for developing, manufacturing, and selling the company's products.

Company Wide Programs

Orientation courses. Almost all business firms provide some kind of formal or informal orientation program. The purpose of the program is to introduce the new employee to the organization— to acquaint him with its policies and goals and to give him some idea of the role he will be expected to assume within it. Generally, the supervisor of a given department will bring together all employees hired within a certain period—say a month, or six weeks—and explain to them the company's policies on such matters as working hours, sick leaves, and fringe benefits. He will also give a brief outline of the company's history and a general description of its major goals. In addition, the new employees may be taken on a tour of the plant, where they may see for themselves the various operations and procedures within the different departments. The tours through the departments may be conducted by the supervisors of those departments, each of whom explains the problems and processes involved in the department's range of operations.

In some cases, formal orientation classes are substituted for the company tour. These classes are generally devoted to surveys of the company's different products and services, each of which is conducted by a "guest lecturer" from the department under discussion. The formal classes which comprise the typical engineering orientation program may last from six weeks to as long as one year. In this period, the new engineers are acquainted with the company's history, its policies, its operations, and its product and services. In addition, they will be given a brief but comprehensive outline of the basic engineering techniques involved in each of the different operations, in an effort to relate their academic training to the procedures they will find in the plant.

Some orientation courses, particularly those designed for new employees in marketing and sales, may last as long as two years; such courses actually constitute a junior executive training program. The new employees attend formal classes in which they are introduced to the company history and policy, sales and marketing techniques, product servicing methods, and sales and engineering. Each participant in the program is "rotated" through the different departments (and different plants, if the company has more than one), spending a given period in each, in order that he may gain a maximum knowledge of the company's over-all operation in the shortest possible time. Such a program is generally under the supervision of the manager of marketing education, who keeps a record of each student's progress as a reference for future counselling and guidance. The advantage of this intensive type of orientation program is that it permits an early evaluation of the employee's potential capacity to deal with the various kinds of functions that constitute the business enterprise. Furthermore, since the new employee generally acts as assistant to the senior salesman or marketing executive in each of the several departments to which he is assigned, the program also allows each employee to make a productive contribution to the company relatively early in his career.

Because the orientation program is designed as much to introduce the new employee to his future work procedures as it is to introduce him to the company, it is generally under the direction of the supervisor of the department in which the new employee is to be located, rather than under the direction of the manager of training and education for the company as a whole. In some companies, however, the orientation program is planned as part of the company's total educational effort, and therefore falls within the area of responsibility of the director or coordinator of training and education. Whichever the pattern adopted, the concept of the orientation program is vital—particularly in the large corporation. The orientation process helps to give the individual an idea of what will be expected of him, an overview of the company's total operation, and a better idea of his part in it. Thus he tends to acquire a greater sense of responsibility for his performance and a stronger commitment to the policies and goals of the company.

Tuition-aid programs.   Many companies offer programs of financial assistance to those employees who voluntarily undertake courses designed to increase their skills or to acquire new skills and knowledge in fields related to their work assignments within the company. The range of courses within a given program depends on the judgment of the coordinator of training and education; in the larger organizations, however, approval is generally forthcoming for any course or degree program indicated by the employee's supervisor as being related to his present job or to his potential development within the company. Usually, any courses required to fulfill the requirements for a high school diploma are given blanket approval, whether or not they are related to the employee's job.

The courses may be taken at any accredited institution, or may be part of an educational program offered by a professional or trade association. In a survey conducted by the National Industrial Conference Board, more than two-thirds of the responding companies indicated that they permitted employees to take correspondence courses.[13]

Company refunds to the employee range from 50 per cent to 100 per cent of tuition charges and other fees; reimbursement is usually contingent upon satisfactory completion of the course. Em-

---

[13] *Personnel Administration in the Small Company,* Studies in Personnel Policy No. 117 (New York: National Industrial Conference Board, 1951).

ployee participation in such plans generally runs at about 5 per cent of eligible employees, with eligibility usually determined on the basis of a minimum length of service. Administration of tuition-aid programs is generally assigned to the personnel department or to the department of education and training.

The tuition-aid program is preferred by some companies because it cuts down on the requirements for teaching staff and educational facilities at the plant. Because payment is contingent on satisfactory completion of the course, the program has a self-selective mechanism: only those employees who are capable of further achievement will go on to profit from the plan. Finally, the adoption of such a plan is an expression of an organization's belief that the self-development of the individual is of benefit not only to him but also the company and to the community.

General education programs. Most large companies offer on-site voluntary educational programs of varying scope which are designed to further the personal development and special abilities of employees. Specific courses are usually organized in response to the expressed interest of a certain number of individuals. The development of the program is generally the responsibility of the co-ordinator of education and training, who also makes arrangements for teaching staff (from within the organization or from nearby schools) and allots funds for instruction costs, textbooks, and supplies.

Classes usually meet after working hours for a weekly two-hour period. The courses, which generally last from twelve to fifteen weeks, are open to all employees; any prerequisites are determined by the nature and level of a given course. The range of courses is indicated in the educational bulletin of one large company:

Business
>   Accounting (7 courses)
>   Office and Secretarial (6 courses)
>   Administration (12 courses)

Technical
>   Mathematics (6 courses)
>   Electricity and Electronics (12 courses)
>   Mechanics and Materials (5 courses)
>   Industrial—Manufacturing (7 courses)
>   Industrial—Production (8 courses)

Engineering
>   Electricity and Electronics (7 courses)

Mathematics and Science (13 courses)
Mechanics and Materials (4 courses)
Computers (5 courses)
Aero-Electronics (7 courses)
Research Aids (1 course)

Personal Development
Effective Speaking
English Review
Report Writing
Speed Reading and Comprehension
Practical Psychology
Effective Communications
Human Relations
Conference Leadership
Introduction to Geophysics
Interviewing Techniques
Psychology of Administration
Techniques of Instruction [14]

General education programs are particularly necessary in plants which are not located near other educational institutions. In any company, however, they are an invaluable aid in raising both the morale and the quality of the staff. The major problem in developing such a program involves discrimination among courses. A number of employees may express an interest in basket-weaving, for example, but it would be difficult to justify the expense of such a course to those who are concerned about educational "frills" and frivolities. Normally the range of courses is determined by the training staff, under the direction of the supervisor of education and training. The standard goal is to provide courses which will improve and increase the employee's specific job abilities and also contribute to their over-all development as individuals.

Special education programs. Nearly every large company offers a program of special education to cover functions which are either highly specialized or of central importance to the company's total operation. Such programs are usually organized in response to a specific request from a functional manager. Classes generally meet during working hours and admission is based on the requirements of a specific course. The program usually includes both on-site and off-site courses.

An example of an on-site special education program would be

---

[14] Oscar N. Serbein, *Educational Activities of Business* (Washington, D.C.: American Council on Education, 1961), p. 98. Used by permission.

one designed to train patent attornies. Most large companies whose products and services are based on advanced and advancing technology have an increasing need for lawyers with scientific or engineering backgrounds. Such companies find it to their interest to provide courses in patent law for those employees with degrees in engineering or science who show an aptitude for this field.

The student attends school part-time, during working hours. During his term of study, he gains practical experience by working on cases selected from the company's own patent operations. Students are expected to supplement their daytime classes by taking part in an evening program of courses leading to a degree in law.

The success of such a program—like that of any educational program—depends on the selection of capable individuals and on an effective method of counselling and guidance during their training period. One danger is that the individual who completes such a program may be tempted to take his new abilities elsewhere. The company that is keeping abreast of technological developments and that develops an educational program in line with its competitive policy goals, however, will have little difficulty in solving this problem.

Correspondence education.   One effective and relatively economical method of providing training and education for the individual in business and industry involves the use of correspondence courses. Correspondence training is not a new phenomenon: some 7,000 concerns are using it or have used it, and more than ten million individuals have taken one or more correspondence courses in their working careers.[15] Today, there are an estimated 800,000 students enrolled in fifty-six accredited schools (See Table VI for distribution among program categories.) Another 700,000 are enrolled in nonaccredited schools, but these will not be dealt with here.[16] And indications are that the rate of enrollment will increase sharply over the next few years.

There has been a tendency in the past to treat correspondence courses lightly, perhaps because many people associate such courses with such well-known ad lines as "I learned to play after only seven lessons," and "I was only a 97-pound weakling, but . . ." Correspondence courses today, however, are not confined to piano-play-

---

[15] *Employee Education,* op. cit.

[16] "Accredited Correspondence Education: An Answer to Training Needs of Business," U.S. Chamber of Commerce *Special Supplement* (Washington, D.C.: November 30, 1962).

TABLE VI

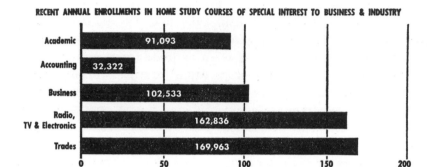

RECENT ANNUAL ENROLLMENTS IN HOME STUDY COURSES OF SPECIAL INTEREST TO BUSINESS & INDUSTRY

This graph provides a comparison of subject area enrollments selected by new students enrolled in accredited home study courses in one year. 558,747 of 860,190 students chose courses vocationally beneficial for working adults.

Source: "Accredited Correspondence Education: An Answer to Training Needs of Business," U.S. Chamber of Commerce *Special Supplement* (Washington, D.C.: November 30, 1962).

ing and muscle-building; rather, they cover a wide range of subjects in technical, vocational, and professional fields. Certainly a major factor in determining the quality of the course is the school or institute that offers it. An independent accrediting commission approved by the U.S. Office of Education sets the following criteria for approving schools:

1. It must have a competent faculty.
2. It must offer educationally sound and up-to-date courses.
3. It must carefully screen applicants.
4. It must provide satisfactory educational services.
5. It must demonstrate student success and satisfaction.
6. It must charge reasonable tuition fees.
7. Its advertising must be truthful and responsible.
8. It must be financially able to deliver a high quality of educacational service.[17]

Schools that meet these requirements report excellent results on their correspondence program. About 90 per cent of the students taking these courses received pay increases averaging $22.50 per

---

[17] *Ibid.*

week; over 40 per cent were promoted or went on to better jobs in other companies.[18]

In practically all large companies and many smaller ones, the employee is reimbursed for all or part of the tuition fees for his correspondence training. The financial aid given by the company to the employee, and its recognition of his satisfactory completion of the training course by an increase in pay or a promotion in rank, helps to increase employee motivation and to stimulate over-all enrollment in correspondence education. The encouragement provided by the company stems largely from the realization that correspondence education provides as many benefits for the employer as it does for the employee. Correspondence education makes it possible for many employees to be trained in many different fields at the same time. Because correspondence courses are pursued largely at home on the employee's own time, the company is not required to provide classrooms, training equipment, or teaching personnel at company expense and on company time. (In some cases, however, correspondence training is incorporated as part of the on-the-job training program.)

For the individual, the correspondence program offers several distinct advantages (in addition to the financial and professional ones mentioned earlier). Because he works at home, he is able to proceed at his own rate of speed. He can devote as much or as little as necessary to difficult problems without feeling that he is being left behind by the rest of the class. Because he has all the study time he needs, his chances for success are correspondingly higher. Finally, the development of programmed instruction, which is particularly appropriate for home study, makes it possible for him to check his answers and discover and correct his own errors. As has been demonstrated in numerous studies, this leads to greater retention of knowledge over a longer period of time.

Correspondence courses are offered by various schools devoted exclusively to home-study education, by high schools, and by colleges and universities. Some of the college and graduate-level courses are planned by the institution in cooperation with the training and education supervisor of a specific company. For instance, IBM developed and administered correspondence courses for its employees: these courses generally covered technical subjects and were designed to allow field employees the same opportunities avail-

---

[18] *Ibid.*

able to plant and laboratory employees through the company's voluntary education classes. In 1961, six of these courses were transferred to Pennsylvania State University, which now offers them as a regular part of its Correspondence Instruction Department. A significant number of IBM employees continue to participate in these courses, aided by the company's tuition refund program.

Many other companies have followed IBM's initial example and have developed their own correspondence programs for field employees. These programs, which typically cover the specification and engineering of new products, the description of new manufacturing processes, or the preparation of sales programs for new products and services, are supervised by the central training department within the company and are open to all qualified employees. In some cases, the program includes classroom sessions or seminars which are designed to supplement the correspondence work of employees within commuting distance of the central offices.

The advantages of correspondence education—the possibility of covering a wide range of material, the relatively low cost, the fact that it need not infringe on the employee's working time, and the fact that it allows each student to work at his own speed and under a minimum of pressure—are such that it must not be ignored by business and industry in their effort to provide employees with the opportunity to enhance their general education background and to improve and increase their technical skills. The successful cooperation of industrial concerns and institutions of high education in offering correspondence courses opens up new possibilities for joint undertakings which will benefit not only the concerns and institutions involved, but also the community as a whole.

Safety education. It is a commonplace that continued work with or near dangerous machinery tends to make the worker careless and occasionally inattentive. With the increasing complexity of modern engineering and technological production processes—their use of high-voltage equipment, volatile substances, heavy machinery, and complicated transfer equipment—even a split-second's distraction may produce serious (even fatal) consequences not only for the individual but also for scores of his fellow workers. The dangers inherent in the modern work process pose a responsibility for management to provide for all employees—from stockboys to the top professional personnel—a thorough and regular program of safety education, designed to teach the proper techniques of accident prevention and fire prevention, and other safety measures.

Safety education programs are generally under the supervision of plant or laboratory safety managers, who work in direct conjunction with the coordinator of training and education. Some companies form safety teams, composed of safety managers from the different sections. These teams then work their way through the various departments of the company, holding one or two-day seminars in each.

Some firms offer formal Red Cross-sponsored safety courses as part of the company voluntary education program. Occasionally this program is combined with the safety team program: the same team that provides safety instruction in the plant and laboratories also provides teachers for and generally supervises the Red Cross course in the program of voluntary education.

Safety education pays an additional dividend: it helps the individual become more conscious of safety requirements in his own home and play environments. Most important, the substantial investment by business in safety education is more than balanced by the costs that might otherwise be incurred by the destruction of expensive equipment and the emotional and financial burden of personal injuries.

CHAPTER V

Educational Programs for Managers

Perhaps the most important educational task in business today—and one, certainly, essential to its continued growth and survival—is the development of its managerial resources. Management development, of course, is a far more inclusive concept than management education. It refers not only to formal courses of instruction but also to the total organizational climate of the firm—the policies and practices that govern the recruitment and selection of employees, their orientation, their periodic appraisal and counselling, their on-the-job training, their promotion and salaries, and even their retirement. Formal programs play only a minor role in the total process of management development. Nevertheless, they make a critical and special contribution by providing explicit recognition of principles, procedures, and practices that are considered to be essential for the successful guidance of the firm. Furthermore, they represent that part of the process that can be shared by industry *with* the universities, thus creating special obligations and opportunities for business in its relationships with institutions of higher education.

The growing importance of management education is a direct result of the increasing complexity of modern business.

> The job of managing . . . is becoming an increasingly . . . taxing assignment. The growth and geographic spread of corporate facilities, the diversification into additional product lines, the high degree of functional specialization have all contributed to placing new challenges upon, and increasing the need for, capable business executives.
>
> These changes are occurring so rapidly that the corporation can no longer afford to wait for managers to "happen." This implies that the corporation can afford to operate a formal program designed to accelerate the development of managers.[1]

One thing is clear: the company that does not devote adequate attention to this crucial area may be seriously limiting its ability to

---

[1] Walter S. Wikstrom, ed., *Developing Better Managers: An Eight-Nation Study* (New York: National Industrial Conference Board, Inc., 1961), pp. 156–57.

grow. It must plan for managerial succession and, at the same time, help the members of the managerial staff to execute their present responsibilities more effectively.

The specific reasons for which a particular company may institute a program of management education vary. In some organizations, the chief motive is to help managers update their knowledge and skills in the areas for which they are responsible. Other companies hope to increase management efficiency and flexibility by exposing executives to new concepts of organization and interpersonal communication. In some cases, a series of mergers or acquisitions may make it necessary for the managerial staff to be introduced to the policies and practices of the parent organization. Companies which are experiencing rapid expansion or undergoing a major reorganization are faced with the need to provide intensive training for those employees who are to take on the new managerial responsibilities thus created. Finally, some companies seek to encourage their executives to undertake more active and effective participation in politics and community affairs and to explore the operations of those federal and state agencies which affect business and government relationships.

Developing an In-Company Program

Assessment of needs. Management education can thus be thought of in very pragmatic terms. Its prime justification is the degree to which it helps to meet the firm's needs for an adequate supply of competent managers over a period of time, whatever other purposes it may be expected to serve.

The first step in planning such a program customarily involves a survey of executive manpower requirements. These studies provide guidelines for the updating of managerial skills and knowledge, the creation of new managerial positions, or the revision of certain structural aspects of the executive establishment. The initial concern may be largely with problems of top management succession, but more and more companies are concerning themselves with the management system as a whole.

Many surveys go further—to a consideration of long-range estimates. These take into account projected company expansion with its concomitant creation of new managerial positions, and the inevitable changes in staff caused by promotions, retirements, transfers, deaths and discharges, and the like.

In other words, educational planning reflects and anticipates the goals established for manpower and organizational needs, for these will determine the size of the group to be educated and the scope of the program to be offered.

Placement in the organizational structure. The significance accorded a formal program of management education is frequently revealed by its location in the organizational structure. Most people agree that the director of management development at first should report directly to the top executive or have opportunity for frequent and regular consultations with him and other top officials of the company. Only in this way will he gain the necessary authority and support and have access to the information which will enable him to maintain a relevant and viable program. The educational function must be perceived as an essential instrument of the chief executive in carrying out his responsibilities for the guidance and direction of the corporation. Although administrative responsibilities may be widely decentralized, the corporate interest must take precedence over divisional or local needs and concerns.

The curriculum. Once the needs are known and the chief executive is committed, course plans can be formulated for the level or levels of management to be engaged in the over-all plan.

As a system evolves it is likely to include at some stage programs for at least four qualitatively different levels of management, each of which presents unique problems. At the top is the senior executive group, the men responsible for the formulation of policy and the general direction of the corporation. Reporting directly to the senior executives is the management group, junior executives who are assigned substantial administrative responsibilities; they can be said to be at the upper levels of middle management and constitute the group from which the future top executives will be selected. A third group is composed of the larger body of middle managers, starting with those who are but one level above the first-line manager up to those who may report to the principal functional and staff managers. The fourth—and largest—management group is made up of the first-line supervisors responsible for the personal direction of groups of employees.

Each of these levels is characterized by clusters of common needs, individual and corporate, and in each case a determination must be made as to which ones can be best met by formal instruction rather than through other avenues of influence and education.

Courses for new first-line managers. Programs for the new

first-line manager are the most common because the need for instruction at this level, however brief, is obvious. As a worker, the individual had been following orders and plans formulated by someone else. Now he has assumed responsibilities which give a new significance to his actions. He must give directions instead of following them; he must make decisions; instead of executing plans, he must formulate them. He must learn how to communicate with others and how to elicit support from his workers. He now shares management's responsibility for the control of costs and profits, and for the larger questions of corporate policy.

Programs for first-line managers vary greatly. They may be centralized or decentralized; they may consist of individual study programs or weekly meetings over a period of several months, or residence programs lasting two or three weeks. A typical program includes four principal parts:

1. Description and discussion of the supervisor's job, and the changes in his role, values, and decisions arising from his new assignment.
2. Analysis of decision-making as a supervisory function.
3. Analysis of personal interrelationships, including problems of supervisory behavior and attitudes, worker motivation, individual needs, and practice in group problem-solving.
4. Analysis of problems of self-development.

A program offered by a large utility company brings new managers together one day a week for nine weeks. Each of the sessions is devoted to the discussion and analysis of one of the following problems:

1. Company history
2. Economics
3. Public power regulations
4. Communications
5. Human relations
6. Accident prevention
7. Labor law
8. Training
9. Decision-making

In one major manufacturing company, new foremen take part in a centralized two-week residence program divided into five units:

1. Analysis of the first-line manager's role.
2. Discussion of the fundamentals of management.
3. Analysis of department functions and interrelationships.
4. Development of management skills and the ability to work with people.
5. Development of management skill in job training and job improvement.

Many of these programs are supplemented by short courses or

special discussion groups, held during working hours, which cover a variety of problems and interests. In one company, for instance, the special course series offered after completion of the basic training program includes sessions on conference leadership, current events, methods analysis, performance appraisal, and principles of industrial engineering.

Almost all programs at this level have three major objectives: to introduce the new manager to his role in the company; to help him understand company policies and practices; and to introduce him to the elements of his new task—working through other people and exercising managerial control.

Courses for middle management. Programs for middle management include some of the topics covered in courses for first-line supervisors, but principal emphasis is placed on the special problems of interfunctional relationships found at this higher level of responsibility. The men moving into middle-management positions must be thoroughly familiar with company and divisional goals, policies, organization, and markets. They must also have the knowledge, the insight, and the ability to manage other managers.

Although there is no consistent pattern of length or content among these programs, most of them are characterized by a combination of the following elements:

1. History of the firm—its philosophy of management and the development of its policies and procedures.
2. Human relations—the problems arising from work relattionships and managerial responsibility.
3. Management policies and practices:
   (a) The problem of organizational forms and their use in managing a complex business structure;
   (b) The importance of marketing strategy and policy in a changing industry;
   (c) The role of financial management in the business enterprise;
   (d) The role of business and its leaders in the society as a whole.

The advanced management courses. Perhaps the most experimental and imaginative of the management development programs are those designed as preparation for top-management positions. The men who occupy these positions are the ones who carry the primary responsibility for formulating company objectives, defining its policies, and developing those procedures which will be most effective in reaching the stated goals.

The programs designed for this level are planned to help participants anticipate the problems inherent in the responsibilities of top management and to develop the new interests and wider perspectives essential for men who will be guiding the future of a corporation.

One interesting example of such a program is that of the IBM Executive School, established in 1957. Its objectives, as set forth by the company, are:

1. To develop in each executive a greater awareness and understanding of, and sensitivity to, the problems of managers and decision-making from a company wide viewpoint;
2. To introduce modern concepts of the business corporation as a dynamic economic system;
3. To develop a deeper understanding of the nature of individual and group behavior within the business organization;
4. To provide a better understanding of the rapidly changing social, political, and economic environment within which business must operate, with particular attention to national goals and purposes;
5. To review the structure of the company, its functional departments and the relationships that exist among them;
6. To develop, through acquaintance and association, a greater spirit of cooperation and understanding among executives in different areas and at different levels;
7. To assist in the identification of men with outstanding qualifications for further promotion.

Although the curriculum has been revised several times to meet changes in company needs and industrial requirements, it has adhered to a series of units based on four general topics:

1. *The business enterprise:* an introduction to modern concepts of the corporation and the analysis of business organizations as economic systems; problems of functional interaction and independence—marketing, engineering, manufacturing, research; executive control and coordination including financial criteria. Special attention is given to the IBM Corporation and its history and emerging needs.
2. *The business environment:* the corporation, the economy and national policy:
   (a) A survey of the American economy—problems of growth, stability, national income accounts, labor and agriculture;
   (b) An introduction to the problems of the modern corporation from the point of view of the manager, the stockholder, the employee, and the community;
   (c) A firsthand study of national policy, the roles of the various branches of the federal government and the development of constructive business-government relations.
3. *The individual and the organization:* a study of individual and group behavior in the large business organization; the effects of change and particularly automation; issues of executive motiva-

tion; planning for effective utilization and development of human resources; the structure and meaning of work in contemporary society; an understanding of effective executive action.

4. *Decision-making:* a variety of experiences in making actual decisions through role-playing, business-simulation exercises and other techniques; stress on analytical methods and the use of new managerial tools, such as operations research.

Top-management course. Although most senior executives prefer to attend out-company programs, some organizations find it effective to provide occasional in-company programs for this group. Such meetings are particularly well-suited for reviewing advances in a company's technology, for analyzing fundamental changes in the company's product line or organization, or for reviewing and evaluating economic, political, and social issues of interest and concern to those charged with the responsibility of shaping long-range plans. An important by-product of such programs is their influence on the other educational activities of the organization. They are clear evidence of top-level commitment to executive development programs for *all* managers.

The Staff

The director. Of utmost importance to the success of the management education function is the selection of an effective director and a competent staff. Because one of the principal objectives of the program is to prepare employees to assume new or larger managerial responsibilities in the organization, the director must be a person who has himself had considerable experience with the firm —and preferably at a relatively high level. He must be thoroughly familiar with the traditions of the company and with its long-range objectives; he must know the written and unwritten rules and practices which govern everyday procedures; he must know and share the interests and concerns of the company's top management. Because the director of the management development program will be working closely with—if he is not directly responsible to—the chief executive officer of the firm, he must be a person who has the full confidence and support of that officer. Because he is to guide the development of the future managers of the company, the director of the program must personify those qualities that the company deems important and must serve as a model for those participating in the program. Above all, he must be a person of vision and flexibility: he must not only support company traditions and, by so doing, stimulate adherence to them, but he must also encourage and provide opportunities for change and growth among those who will one day be responsible for the direction and continuing viability of the firm. If men of this calibre and experience are to be attracted to work of this kind, their role must be clearly established within the top ranks of the corporate staff with provision for a close working relationship with the head of the firm.

The administrative staff. The factor of organizational recognition is also a fundamental condition for the recruitment of a strong staff group. Their number and their qualifications will depend, of course, on the objectives of the program. Is the program designed to cover several managerial groups, or is it to be confined to a specific management level? Is the program to be administered at a central location, or at a number of different plant and field facilities? Is the program a terminal undertaking designed to fill current needs, or is it to be conducted on a continuing basis to provide a constant flow of managerial candidates? Upon the answers to these fundamental questions depends the selection of the management development staff. The more numerous and comprehensive the objectives of the program, the larger and more highly qualified will be the staff required for its administration.

Whatever the size of the program, most of the staff members—like the director—must be persons of wide experience in business generally and especially with the particular firm. Because they too are, in a sense, models for the participants in the program, they must display those qualities deemed important by the company. They must also be completely familiar with its operating policies and procedures and, in addition, they must have a degree of expertness in a particular functional area.

The administrative and teaching staff preferably should not be composed of salesmen, managers, and production men exclusively. No matter how effective these people may have been in their respective fields, their business experience has usually not been of a nature to equip them to organize a series of courses and to teach a subject systematically. Few of them have had the time or the inclination to keep up with current research. The business background and experience these people bring to the management development program is indispensable, but it must be supplemented by knowledge from other professional fields.

Specialists in curriculum planning, for example, have proven to be especially helpful. There may also be a place for the expert in psychological testing and evaluation. In any case, it is customary to include on the management development staff one or more professional educators who have had experience in working with adults, who are familiar with the structure and organization of the materials that form the content of the courses, and who are capable of planning and developing a coherent course of instruction that will meet the over-all objectives of the program. Sometimes these specialists are to be found within the corporation itself—particularly if it is a large one. More often, however, they are drawn from the universities, either as temporary consultants or as staff advisors to be associated with a particular project over an extended period of time.

The teaching staff. The addition of "outside" instructors normally enhances the quality of the program and widens the perspectives of the participants. The person designated to assume an ever-widening range of managerial responsibilities needs a knowledge of practices, procedures, and opinions in other companies and in other industries as well as his own. If he is to acquire this knowledge and perspective, he must be exposed to a staff composed of people who offer different types of experience and who display different—perhaps even conflicting—viewpoints. Outside consultants can offer a challenge to traditional positions without fear of endangering their own professional status. By the same token, they can provide an objective criticism of the individual participant's reaction to a particular problem—a criticism which carries no threat, open or implied, to his security or status within the company. Only under these conditions can the program break the bonds of intracompany parochialism and provide the intellectual breadth and flexibility essential to creative management.

Staff stability and continuity are also important considerations which will have an effect on selection. Frequent changes in staff make it difficult for ideas to develop or plans to mature. And the atmosphere of impermanence thus created can have only a detrimental effect on the program as a whole. Staff turnover represents a constant problem for company staff directors. One reason is that many of those who are assigned to the educational function in business regard it as a temporary or transitional phase in their careers. Their motivation arises from external stimuli rather than from a personal commitment to teaching. Those few who choose, or are chosen, to devote themselves to educational careers in business are usually thought of as minor functionaries: opportunities for promotion are few and far between: recognition—professional or financial—often falls far short of their contributions to the organization.

This attitude is reflected in the nature and length of teaching appointments. If the course is a brief one and offered at long intervals, the person assigned to teach it may return to his original position at the end of each session. If the course is longer, or offered more frequently, the teaching appointment may extend over a period of one to three years, or perhaps even longer.

Outside consultants usually serve as part-time staff members. There is no general pattern established for such appointments. Often the arrangement is quite informal, with the consultant serving on a per diem basis.

In addition, there are certain key executives in the corporation who, as a function of their office, regularly participate in management development programs and who therefore are in every sense members of the part-time teaching staff. Other company executives may be invited to participate from time to time as part of a rotational scheme designed to introduce as many management-level personnel as possible to the activities and objectives of the educational program.

The total staff participating in a four or five-week program, for example, may come to thirty or forty people, including full and part-time instructors and special guest discussion leaders. The effective coordination of such a group is probably the chief task of the staff director.

Evaluation. The special circumstances and conditions of education in business and industry make it difficult to evaluate the instruction and instructors in a management development program. The instructor's general knowledge of his field is presumably established at the time of his appointment to the teaching staff. The critical point, then, is his ability to communicate effectively with his students. Accordingly, the principal method of appraising instruction is to elicit student reactions. They may be asked to fill out a complex rating form or, more simply, to assign a value along a five-point scale (i.e. 5: Excellent; 4: Above Average; 3: Satisfactory; 2: Below Average; 1: Poor), or merely to comment briefly on their reactions. If several groups give a particular instructor a "below average" or "poor" rating, his appointment is usually terminated if he is not able to improve his performance. Such rating methods are admittedly far from ideal, but if thoughtful responses are encouraged, the procedure helps to assure good standards of teaching.

Teaching methods and schedules. Although management courses in business tend to be conservative and conforming in content, a generous eclectism seems to prevail in approaches to teaching. The major goal is to encourage and stimulate student involvement through discussion, but the traditional lecture has not been abandoned.

Schedules tend to be extraordinarily heavy: five or six class hours a day, plus as many more hours of individual reading and preparation. Programs are clearly not disguised vacations: the participants' work day is as long or longer than that put in on their regular jobs. Intensive schedules are, perhaps, unavoidable, but they present a serious drawback by failing to provide enough time for private reflection and independent reading.

There is wide use of audio-visual techniques. Programmed learning is being adopted by more and more companies. There is also heavy reliance on preparatory reading, case study and problem analysis and on small group discussion. There is understandably a great emphasis on decision-making experiences both in discussions and in business simulation games.

Business firms who devote a lot of attention to executive development are continually concerned with the task of giving their promising men over-all perspective and both diversified and specialized experience. When a man moves up to a position of greater responsibility, it is usually expected that he will make a few mistakes. That's part of the risk, and how big it is depends largely on the man himself.

One way of providing some of the much-desired view from the top with no risk at all is by simulation of business management using a computer. A business game consists of a set of procedures, accounting and operating reports, and a model of the business, all of which are operated within a computer program. In establishing a model the assumptions can be as detailed or as broad as the trainer wishes. Since the technique was first developed seven years ago, thousands of people have played "management games," either on their own organization's computers or those of a computer center or manufacturer. These people have held positions ranging from first-line and middle-management groups up to top management levels.

They have practiced decision-making in an environment where

several years of certain kinds of business activity can be concentrated into a few hours of quarterly business decisions and annual reports printed out by a computer. They have deepened their managerial capacities much as an airline pilot hones his flying skills by practicing in a ground device for simulating instrument flying.

Practically all the features of running a business in a competitive environment are present. And the models can be as simple or as complex as desired. The time taken to "play" the game can run from less than a day to an entire college semester or year. The number of decisions to be made can range from a dozen to several hundred.

In a relatively simple game, participants make judgments on pricing and allocating funds for production, plant improvement, research, and marketing.

Many authorities now regard the management game as important a tool for the education of business careerists as the case method, seminars, lectures, and appropriate summer employment. Indeed, it has been estimated that more than 100 universities today are using variations of the management game in under-graduate or graduate business or engineering courses. The nature of the exercise focuses on the nub of all business enterprise: profit and loss, where the success or failure of business is measured.

Student Personnel Policies and Procedures

Eligibility and selection of participants. Candidates for the more important management development programs are usually selected, or referred for approval, by top-level management. In some cases, an employee may become eligible for enrollment in a course of study immediately upon his promotion to a particular managerial position. Candidates for the more advanced programs, however, are usually chosen on the basis of outstanding potential for high-level management responsibilities, provided they also meet certain age requirements. Typically, they must be in their late thirties or early forties.

Evaluation of participants. The issue of student accountability is a matter of some controversy. Most companies consciously avoid the process of student evaluation. Those opposed argue that such a procedure tends to introduce unnecessary tension and stress into an atmosphere designed to encourage self-development and self-evaluation. They also maintain that the brevity of the typical course does not allow time for a fair and objective judgment and that the observations made in the classroom are not relevant to appraisals of managerial potential.

Those few companies which undertake to evaluate participants are interested in information that will assist in determining promotions and in providing guidelines for the best use of their executive resources. One company uses a peer evaluation technique, with the participants anonymously evaluating one another. This device is supplemented by objective tests, and the observations and judgments of the teaching staff. Whatever the technique used, the data it supplies must be carefully interpreted. Equally important: the results should be made available only to those authorized senior executives upon whom rests the responsibility for such decision.

Educational facilities. A decision which must be made fairly early in the planning of the management development program is the physical location of the educational center or centers. When the program is designed to bring together executives from different divisions so that they may study interdepartmental and interfunctional relationships, a central facility is usually provided. If, on the other hand, the program is designed to train first-line supervisors, who will be principally involved in problems which are local in origin or in manifestation, it is more efficient to use a number of educational facilities in different areas. The final choice usually depends on company policy and on the resources available.

Most large corporations tend to favor suburban or campus sites. General Electric, for instance, has a management development center in Westchester County, near New York City; IBM brings its executives to a country setting on the North Shore of Long Island; the Bell System seems to favor college campuses—Dartmouth, Williams, Swarthmore, Northwestern, Carlton; and a number of corporations find that the inns in Princeton, New Jersey, provide an atmosphere conducive to intellectual effort.

Out-Company Programs

Since World War II, more and more corporations have supplemented their own educational and training activities by encouraging selected employees—particularly higher-level executives—to participate in programs of study offered by universities and various professional organizations such as the American Management Association. The demand for these programs can be traced to World

War II experiences, especially at the Harvard Business School, which demonstrated the effectiveness of short training courses in functional management. Once reconstituted the programs have moved far beyond the limited objectives originally sought by industry. For example, the many programs sponsored by the Columbia University Graduate School of Business at Arden House include sessions for top management, for international management and for executives of special industry groups.

These programs, customarily described as out-company programs, may be classified according to location, content, method of instruction, technique, size and nature of enrollment, or cost. The more important programs, however, can probably best be described according to their philosophy and principal objective. Under this criterion, there are three general types of programs:

1. Those devoted largely to questions of business policy and the intensive study of functional problems.
2. Those drawing heavily on the liberal arts and sciences.
3. Those designed to improve the quality of membership in groups and organizations.

There are outstanding examples of each type, but what may be of greater significance is a trend among the more comprehensive programs to integrate two—or even all three—of these approaches. The Advanced Management Program of the Harvard Business School, for instance, although primarily an example of the first category, displays characteristics of all three. Its professed goals are:

1. Broader comprehension of the economic, political, social, and technical dimensions of the many changes sweeping rapidly across the national and international scene;
2. Greater competence in casting realistic and promising over-all plans effectively geared to rapidly evolving trends . . . ;
3. Increased understanding of the processes whereby the various functional aspects of a modern organization can be integrated into an effective, dynamic whole;
4. Greater perception and knowledge of the human aspect of organizations;
5. Increased awareness of the growing array of procedures whereby they may more effectively perceive, evaluate, and respond to developing changes in opportunities;
6. A reinforced foundation for the manager's continuing education . . . ;
7. Further understanding of the managers' responsibility toward their society and environment . . . ;

8. A more effective concern for thinking and acting in ways which will enrich . . . (the managers') own lives.[2]

There are those, however, who believe the needs of the top executive, in fact of any executive, can be best provided for in courses of liberal philosophy and content. Examples of this approach are the Executive Seminars of the Aspen Institute for Humanistic Studies, the conferences for business executives conducted by The Brookings Institution, and the Program in American Studies for Executives at Williams College.

Students at Aspen participate in two weeks of lectures and discussions designed to develop the executive's understanding of his role in society, the possible goals toward which he may direct his organization, and his own influence upon it. Because the over-all aim is to widen and deepen the executive's intellectual base, the program is built around the great works of the world's leading philosophers, economists, historians, and political leaders—past and present. (It is interesting to note that the wives of the participating executives are also encouraged to attend these sessions.)

The one-week program offered by The Brookings Institution in Washington, D.C., is designed to expose the executive to key operations of the federal government. Participants in the program meet with leaders in the three branches of government, and analyze and discuss problems of concern both to business and to government. Most of the sessions are conducted in the offices of government agencies and departments or on Capitol Hill, and the fact that the sessions are off the record tends greatly to encourage a free exchange of views.

Williams College offers a six-week program devoted to a study of American political thought and constitutional law, American philosophy, religion, and ethics, as well as American architecture, literature, and art. The program, designed to contribute to the participants' personal maturity and executive effectiveness, also places great emphasis on discussions of the national problems posed by economic development and foreign policy.

The significance of these programs has been characterized as follows:

First, they represent industry's increasing awareness that merely technically trained personnel are not adequate to meet industry's changing needs. Industry demands not only specialists and "broad

[2] From the 1963–64 announcement of the Advanced Management Program of the Harvard University Graduate School of Business Administration, Boston, Mass.

gauged" persons but also those who are both specialists *and* broad gauged.

Second, they demonstrate a growing concern on the part of both industry and academia for developing persons who, for the good of the society, must have their horizons broadened and their lives enriched for the new leisure and for changing, growing responsibilities as citizens.

Third, they indicate some validity to the idea that liberal education can, for many people, more profitably come *after* specialized training and years of experience on the specialized job rather than *before*.

Fourth, they give credence to the assumption that a special kind of program must be developed for the person who has had a broad living experience which must be taken into account as an important dimension in adult education.

Fifth, they make clear the growing tendency to look upon *liberal education* as the way to achieve a much-needed base for personal growth.

These programs indicate that business, industry, and academia have committed themselves to a third phase of in-service education for the new era. If the first phase was the provision of specific technical training either in company-owned schools or outside, and if the second phase can be considered the broadened over-all business-management education in the manner of the Harvard Advanced Management program or the University of Chicago Executive Program, then the third phase is the development of the liberal arts programs we see mushrooming all over the country.[3]

The third category of programs comprise those designed to improve the quality of the participants' membership in groups and organizations, providing what has come to be known as "sensitivity training."

One such program is that offered by the National Training Laboratories of the National Education Association, which uses laboratory or group training methods to help individuals learn to cope more effectively with small-group, and organizational decision-making problems. Its leaders assert that:

> Highly complex problems require a high level of skill, sensitivity, and competence. Conventional training approaches (lectures, discussions, demonstrations) can provide important information and influence attitudes without actually changing ways of behaving. People often *know* better than they *do*. Effective training for action has to work simultaneously at the levels of *knowing, doing,* and *feeling.*[4]

[3] Peter E. Siegle, *New Directions in Liberal Education for Executives* (Chicago: Center for the Study of Liberal Education for Adults, 1958), pp. 1, 2.

[4] From the 1964 announcement of the Fifth Annual Laboratories for Community Leadership Training, National Training Laboratories, National Education Association, Washington, D.C.

The participants in the program learn to build work groups that can set goals, define problems, communicate with other groups, and develop leadership. The knowledge, new perceptions, and new behaviors acquired through the laboratory experience can then be applied to real-life situations in which the same skills and sensitivities are needed.

Evaluation. Out-company programs are as difficult to evaluate as any other educational experience in business. The responses of participants almost uniformly provide an overwhelming endorsement of the value of such programs to the individual, but such reactions offer no indication of the relative merit of the different programs, or of the different types of programs. From the organization's point of view, it is difficult to judge whether the executive might not have developed the same skills, knowledge, and sensitivity through prolonged exposure to his new responsibilities. As for the participants themselves, the simple fact of having been selected to take part in such a program is interpreted as a mark of prestige, perhaps even an end in itself. There is little evidence or documentation of changes in attitude or perspective, or of attainment of new knowledge and skills.

Present methods of evaluation are, for the most part, highly subjective and limited in scope. The programs are usually studied as discrete entities, rather than as one of a series of developmental experiences. To be properly evaluated, these programs should be studied as part of a larger effort to combat corporate provincialism and complacency and to provide opportunities for withdrawal and reflection as well as for commitment and redirection.

The corporation derives maximum benefit from out-company programs when it is able to choose the appropriate program for a particular individual at a given stage of his career. Obviously, such programs must not be chosen on the basis of the pleasantness of their location. Nor must participants be chosen on the basis of availability, expendability, or length of service. Participation in an out-company program should not be regarded either as a status symbol or as an extended vacation. Such programs are most effective when appropriate criteria have been established for the choice of program and the selection of participants. This task is facilitated when sponsoring institutions exercise their proper responsibility in the establishment of admissions requirements. Although the respective development contributions of the corporation and university have not yet been properly articulated, both are coming to realize the importance of cooperation in the total development of the individual executive.

Reintegration. A particular problem posed by out-company programs is the reintegration of the individual with his new attitudes and skills. Because most of these courses call for brief but intensive participation, the students must devote nearly all their time to fulfilling the daily assignments. There is little opportunity for the private thought and reflection essential to the assimilation of new concepts and ideas.

Two solutions to this problem have been suggested. One would provide for the last three or four days of each program to be devoted to a general review and summary of the material covered. Each participant would take part in this informal but comprehensive examination, and consider the relevance of certain ideas for his own area of activity. The alternative is to allow the participants some free time after the end of the program, before they return to work. They would make use of this interval to analyze their impressions, examine those ideas which seem to have the greatest applicability to their work, and consider how these new ideas and approaches might be effectively and efficiently introduced into their own organizations.

Whatever their present defects, it is clear that management development programs of every kind are essential to the progress of business and industry in the United States. All the large corporations—and many of the smaller firms—are coming to realize that experience may not always be the best teacher.

Looking to the future, however, a better division of labor between industry and unversities would seem to be desirable. As Kenneth Andrews of the Harvard Business School has suggested internal company programs might well concentrate "on teaching competitive and other environmental facts of life peculiar to that corporation. Functional subjects—marketing, accounting, etc.—should be taught either in the company or in specialized university programs. Then universities offering the broad, general courses could assume prior knowledge of these subjects."[5] Whatever the direction that will be taken, the emergence of management development programs since World War II has been a remarkable phenomenon, a response to a society in which the life of intellect and the life of action form two poles.

---

[5] Reported in article on "Why Businessmen Go Back to School," *Business Week,* April 27, 1963, p. 50.

CHAPTER VI

Evaluations and Projections

Education and Economic Growth

The most compelling justification for the educational activities of business and industry lies in their positive relationship to economic growth. The pressures of national and international competition have made the success of the individual firm—and the health of the economy as a whole—dependent upon the ability to develop and utilize fully the knowledge and skills of those who constitute the labor force of the nation.

The problem of development and utilization is complicated by the inescapable fact of obsolescence. Knowledge and skills, as well as machines, are becoming more and more quickly outdated. The same technological explosion which renders obsolete the knowledge of the graduate engineer within ten years after he leaves the university has begun to affect every level of the production process and the people involved in it. Yet both the explosion and its fruits are essential to economic survival.

If current advances in science and technology are to continue, if the individual worker is to acquire and perfect the skills needed on the labor market, if the national economy is to thrive and expand—then industry, the universities, and the government must work together to provide the resources, the materials, and the incentive needed for a comprehensive program of continuing education.

Although the concept of continuing education is now widely accepted, its implementation still leaves much to be desired. Hundreds of programs are being offered by countless business firms, universities, and professional organizations. Taken together, however, they fail to form a coherent and significant pattern. There is no uniformity of content, instruction, organizational responsibility, or educational goals. And, on the whole, only among the larger corporations is there a constant and systematic encouragement of employees to take advantage of the educational opportunities at hand.

Far more disturbing than the inevitable existence of these problems is the lack of research activity devoted to discovering their solutions. Perhaps the most logical point of origin for these research programs would be the universities, which have the benefit of established departments of education and social science, and of professional staffs well-versed in laboratory and research techniques. But it remains for business leaders to stress the need for these programs, and for business and government together to supply the incentive and the funds for this undertaking.

Areas for Research

Curriculum. The area in need of the most rigorous examination is the curriculum itself, its construction and its evaluation. Any program is good, bad, or indifferent only in relation to its effectiveness in meeting the objectives which underlie its conception. The construction and evaluation of any curriculum, therefore, must be preceded by the formulation and articulation of specific educational goals. Why is a program to be offered? What is it to consist of? Who will participate in it? What is it designed to achieve? By whom will it be evaluated—by the participants? by management? by the teaching staff? These are the questions to which carefully planned and adequately financed research may provide answers. This concern is also shared by some critics in the universities. Harold J. Leavitt has asserted that:

> Management development programs need . . . to be oriented much more toward the future, toward change, toward differences from current forms of practice and behavior. We have been moving rapidly in this direction in the better business schools, stimulated by the Ford and Carnegie reports on business education. We have been changing curriculums at a great clip, and the changes have been essentially away from the teaching of current practice toward the teaching of tools and knowledge for changing current practice. We are finally knocking much of the fluff out of our campus programs. But the change has not penetrated very far into our executive development programs. There we are proceeding with much more caution, much more concern about upsetting our students by asking then to think about unfamiliar problems or difficult issues. We have devoted enormous, almost ludicrous amounts of energy to the physical and social amenities in such programs, the food and the status levels of the participants and their interactions. We have often used the participative beliefs as our rationale for these concerns. But as all of us in the academic world know, there are many other good reasons for wanting to have our school's executive program populated entirely by presidents of large corporations. And so we have

been extremely cautious about making senior executives unhappy by
serving them overtough steaks or ideas.

As educators and academicians most of us are convinced that we
have knowledge and methods that can lead current managerial practice by a good many years. It then seems downright immoral to work
so hard to mute and soften our explication of those ideas when the
same energy might better go toward developing them.[1]

The vast increase in knowledge and information has direct relevance for problems of training and management, thus posing a constant need for curriculum revision by educators in industry as well
as those in the schools and colleges. For example, although the
principal focus of management education has traditionally been on
such major functional areas as marketing, production, and finance,
there is now a growing emphasis on the behavioral sciences, management science, business games, and sensitivity training, as well as
a new interest in problems of business ethics and business-government relationships.

A new problem has been created by the growth of the international corporations. They exert a direct or indirect influence over national economic policies, and their capital investments affect—and
sometimes determine—the international balance of payments. The
presence and importance of these organizations creates new needs
for curriculum revision. Intensive courses in international affairs
are essential for men who are being prepared for overseas assignments and for the increasing number of corporate managers whose
responsibilities and opportunities transcend regional or national
boundaries. This is clearly an area in which industry and the universities must work closely together.

Another important area of curriculum revision involves the behavioral sciences, the significance of which is still not adequately
understood by many business leaders today. Mason Haire has suggested that communication between theorists and practitioners
might be improved by the establishment of "developmental research" centers in which scientists would be free to test their theories
comprehensively and systematically. These "learning laboratories"
would be set up within—or in close cooperation with—business
firms and would deal with problems relevant to the business community. Haire, and others who agree with him, maintain that such

---

[1] Harold J. Leavitt, *Unhuman Organizations,* a paper prepared for the Centennial Symposium on Executive Development, School of Industrial Management,
Massachusetts Institute of Technology, Cambridge, Massachusetts, April 27–29,
1961, p. 33–34.

programs might give rise to a revolution of productivity in industry, exceeding that which has taken place in agriculture over the past half-century.

Business education courses also need to give more attention to the liberal arts. Many of the problems of the business community are related to questions of economic, social, and ethical values which transcend technical considerations. Management development programs have begun to emphasize the value of the liberal arts at the executive level; it remains for business leaders to realize that a wider background in the liberal arts would enrich the personal and professional lives of all members of the labor force.

Educational methods and the learning process. A great need also exists for studies of educational methods, particularly as these refer to the learning process among adults. Industry, to its great credit, has been generally more willing to experiment with new teaching approaches than have most schools or colleges, but its investment in the study and evaluation of these methods, unfortunately, has been negligible. Only a program of systematic research will point out the relative merits of such educational techniques as lectures, discussion groups, seminars, programmed instruction, role-playing, business games, and case studies. Because an indispensable component of any educational program is the participant's involvement in the learning process, it is essential that the special characteristics of the adult learner in the industrial establishment be examined and analyzed. Such an analysis may help to provide answers to questions of motivation, authority relationships, incentive and reward systems, and many other aspects of corporate life which have relevance for the learning process.

Costs and budgets. Another important area of research involves the economics of education within the business environment. It is important that simple accounting procedures be established to determine which costs may properly be charged to the educational function and which should constitute direct (rather than indirect) expenditures. Some method might also be devised to measure the value accruing from the educational program in terms of increased worker productivity, reduced absenteeism, or more effective intra-company communication. Finally, there should be some way of estimating the contribution of educational activities to the general welfare of the organization and its capacity for growth and innovation.

The teaching staff. The problems of teachers—and teaching—

in a business environment have been stressed in earlier chapters. Certainly no educational enterprise can be successful if it lacks a well-trained and well-motivated teaching staff. There is an urgent need for research on the policies governing the selection and appointment of teachers in industry. What background is required of prospective teachers? Is teacher training important? What are the most effective forms of recognition and compensation in this field? Are there any opportunities for advanced study? The answers to questions such as these may help to establish guide lines and criteria that will assure an educational program of the highest possible quality.

Cooperation with the schools and universities.   The changing nature of the work process has made inevitable, and will eventually make more pressing, the need for the continuing education of the individual worker. To meet its responsibilities in this area, industry will have to establish and expand more formal educational programs. The growth in number and scope of these programs will tend to place a new and important emphasis on the education departments within the management structure. The recruitment of staff members for these departments, the problems of organization and finance, and the relationship of these departments to the company's general goals and objectives are, as has been seen, even now important considerations for management.

The solution to some of these problems might well lie in closer cooperation between the educational personnel in business and industry and their counterparts in public and higher education. Much of the work and many of the ideas developed in the schools and universities would prove valuable in the development of policies and practices for education in business and industry. And the benefits would be reciprocal: the new concept of education as an investment, an outgrowth of the economic thinking characteristic of industry, will provide new and practical approaches to the financing of public and higher education. It is thus in the interests of all those involved in education to seek methods of beginning and extending a dialogue which will ultimately strengthen education both in business and in the schools.

Individualized education.   The gradual differentiation of programs of management development marks a desirable trend toward individualized education. But programs at all levels, in-company and out-company, would benefit from an evaluation made in terms of the needs of the individual. It would, of course, be unrealistic to suggest that corporations might construct their educational activities on the tutorial system, but there are two other devices which would achieve much the same effect though more efficiently and less expensively.

The first—the technique of programmed, or computer-assisted instruction—has already begun to be explored in the schools and universities. Its intelligent use may well be a factor in changing much of modern education. The use of electronic computers has made possible the recording of vast sums of knowledge in relatively minute storage areas, and has greatly facilitated the individual's access to any specific piece of information. From the educational point of view, perhaps the most important characteristic of programmed instruction is that it allows the individual learner to proceed at his own pace. Freedom from the pressure of competition with fellow-students has been found to enhance and speed learning. And because the system permits the student to discern and correct his own errors, he has a clear and constant indication of the progress he is making, and a far greater sense of responsibility for his own participation in the learning process.

Programmed instruction also allows a more effective use of teaching resources because students using such a system would require a minimum of guidance and supervision, the teachers would be free to devote particular attention to those individuals who had demonstrated a need for remedial help or counseling.

One final advantage of programmed education is its wide applicability in the business world. Properly supplemented by audio-visual or live demonstrations, it can be used to teach many manual or technical skills. And its increasing acceptance in many institutions of higher education is an indication of its effectiveness in providing the broad general education base which has become indispensable to workers at every level of responsibility.

On the managerial level, the corporation might find it profitable to experiment with "executive sabbaticals." The universities have traditionally found it to their own advantage to allow teachers to take every seventh year in order to expand their knowledge and refresh their impressions. By the same token, it might not be unreasonable for a company to encourage a promising young executive to interrupt his business career for a period of several months and spend the time at a university, pursuing studies of his own choosing, or which have a direct relationship to his professional duties. A plan of this kind would, of course, be expensive, but the returns—in terms of individual growth and satisfaction—would be correspondingly high.

Evaluation. The problem of evaluating the merit of an educational program or an individual's progress within it has already been emphasized. Ostensibly the lack of evaluative reports to supervisors frees the participants in educational programs from normal business pressures and thus increases their willingness to take part in such programs. A few firms, however, have come to believe that any negative aspects of formal evaluation would be more than offset by the increase in motivation and the improvement of over-all performance that would follow its introduction. The forms of evaluation usually proposed include extensive reports of performance in class and summaries of personal and intellectual qualities considered relevant to future managerial performance. Some method of measurement is certainly necessary, particularly in programs designed to identify and develop candidates for promotion to higher levels of responsibility. More research is needed, however, to determine the validity and reliability of the various forms of measurement and evaluation, and the areas in which they may be most appropriately applied.

Education for leadership and creativity. A number of books published over the past few years attest to the growing concern with education for business leadership. Among these were the 1959 studies of the collegiate schools of business, sponsored by the Ford Foundation and the Carnegie Corporation of New York; the various reports of the Institute of Higher Education, Teachers College, Columbia University, on the relationship between professional education and the liberal arts; and a series of papers published by the Industrial Relations Section, Princeton University, on the problems of national manpower policy.[2]

These and other studies in the field reveal that education for leadership—especially creative leadership—is rarely seen in its full dimensions. Special courses or isolated experiences designed to in-

[2] R. A. Gordon and J. E. Howell, *Higher Education for Business* (New York: Columbia University Press), 1959; Frank C. Pierson, *The Education of American Businessmen: A Study of University and College Programs in Business Administration* (New York: McGraw-Hill Book Company), 1959; J. Douglas Brown and Frederick Harbison, *High-Talent Manpower for Science and Industry,* Industrial Relations Section (Princeton University, Department of Economics and Sociology), 1957; *Liberal Education and Business* (from "Selected Issues in Higher Education"), William M. Kephart, James E. McNulty and Earl J. McGrath, Institute of Higher Education, Teachers College Press, Columbia University.

culcate these qualities fall far short of the objectives: the results are, at best, short-lived.

The development of an effective program of education must be based on the realization that education is a continuous process. The recruitment and selection of employees, their early assignments, the quality of supervision, the system of monetary and non-monetary rewards, the degree of freedom and responsibility granted—all provide opportunities for informal instruction. The need for and relevance of formal educational programs must be determined within this larger context of informal learning, and must be so designed as to supplement and reinforce the educational experiences inherent in the modern corporate system.

As J. Douglas Brown points out:

> Creativity arises not from *techniques,* but from a *climate* of the mind and spirit . . . It is a mysterious power of association of ideas, of bits and pieces of knowledge, of questions, hunches, and imagined premises.
> Intuition thrives in a free-wheeling climate in which sensitivity, clarity, and association work both consciously and unconsciously and not under the severe restraints of logic or precedent. The enrichment by diverse sources of association and the stimulation of the mind by many elements of climate seem to produce the greater results.[3]

One advantage enjoyed by the business community is that it is not bound by the rigid educational traditions which prevail in the academic world. The educator in business is far more free to try new methods of instruction and different curricular combinations. Yet too few business organizations exploit this unique advantage. Many of the programs offered attempt to lay the intellectual foundation for a professional movement, but make no provision for differences in individual and corporate needs. The more flexible and diversified approach essential to the creation of a "climate of creativity" may possibly be more expensive, but it will undoubtedly be more productive.

These are but a few of the problem areas in business education in which systematic programs of research and evaluation are needed and would prove beneficial. But if these programs are to be undertaken, some way must first be found to bridge the gap between the business community and the academic world. Effective research

---

[3] J. Douglas Brown, "University Perspective—Education for Leadership," *University, A Princeton Publication,* Summer 1964, No. 21, p. 1.

programs will require the guidance of people who can serve as intermediaries between the two systems—independent consultants or special staff members attached either to business or to the campus. The process of interaction and communication can also be facilitated through the use of conferences and joint committees representing both the business and academic sectors. These and other forms of cooperation will be necessary to the initiation and execution of research programs and to the application of research findings to the educational problems of business.

New Educational Responsibilities of Business

National manpower development programs. A business firm undertakes educational activities primarily to meet its own training and retraining needs but, in the aggregate, these activities represent an important contribution to the solution of the nation's more difficult manpower problems. Industry's apprenticeship programs, for instance, continue to provide a major source of formal training for many skilled manual occupations. Government's increasing awareness of the relationship between education, employment, and productivity has led it to depend more and more upon industry for assistance in attacking the problems of an expanding economy.

Under the Manpower Development and Training Act of 1962, companies in many different localities have joined forces in establishing or expanding community on-the-job training programs. Several large corporations have entered into contracts with the U.S. Office of Economic Opportunity to establish job-training centers for the growing number of unskilled, unemployable school dropouts.

The weaknesses and inflexibility of school programs devoted to vocational and work education were sharply revealed during the 1930's. When the New Deal sought to assist youth in preparing for some degree of vocational competence, it found itself forced to create new agencies outside the educational establishment—the Civilian Conservation Corps (CCC) and the National Youth Administration (NYA). Simultaneously there was a small but significant volunteer work camp movement sponsored by private agencies. More than 4 million people were connected with these programs and the resources of the country—human and natural—were conserved and strengthened through their efforts.

The CCC, founded in 1933, had as it original purpose the provision of work relief for young men unable to find regular employment. As the needs of the enrollees became better understood over the years, the original purposes were expanded and by 1939 President Roosevelt, in a message to Congress, commented that "its major purpose is to promote the welfare and further training of the individuals who make up the Corps, important as may be the construction work which they carry on so successfully."

The NYA was established in 1935 to help those young men who were not able to leave their communities to attend the camps and young women, who were not eligible to join. At first, part-time work projects were offered for young people in their own communities. Later, resident centers were established—first in rural areas, and then in or near cities, to provide specialized training for industrial and mechanical occupations.

In spite of the enormous success of these programs, they were discontinued during the war years. Only now are they beginning to re-emerge in a somewhat different form as a part of the Johnson Administration's program for helping disadvantaged youth attain the skills necessary for employment. The training camps that are now being set up in different parts of the country under the Job Corps draw much of their inspiration from the earlier New Deal projects. They also are a reminder that our established educational institutions, even with the greater latitude provided under the Vocational Education Act of 1963, are not yet equipped to deal with some of the more difficult developmental needs of youth. Further, the introduction to the business and industrial milieu of young people from diverse socio-ecomonic and cultural backgrounds poses subtle educational problems. Under our revitalized national commitment to equality of opportunity these are being considered anew. Thoughtful programs must be organized to guarantee the individual maximum opportunity to learn the skills, attitudes and value systems characterizing the business world.

A significant characteristic of the present programs is the unique emphasis placed upon the participation of business and industry. For example, some individual companies, under contract with the Office of Economic Opportunity, are charged with the organization and administration of Job Training Centers. They are responsible for developing the instructional program, selecting the staff, and providing living facilities for the students. The program also provides for participation by institutions of higher education in such areas as educational administration, program evaluation, and research. The implications of this new dimension of private corporate education in the public interest are intriguing, but their full significance probably will not become clear for several years to come.

Neil W. Chamberlain, professor of economics at Yale University, has suggested that we should begin to think of "the corporation as a college." Writing in the June 1965 issue of *The Atlantic* he points out that industry has, in addition to its technical, plant, and financial resources, large numbers of highly educated and trained employees able to instruct, perhaps as part of their work. These are people who should be properly considered as an essential part of our total supply of teachers. Large companies could staff programs of great variety, while smaller companies could operate joint enterprises. These programs could be offered at the elementary, intermediate or advanced levels. The universities would continue to offer supplementary instruction and invaluable services in curriculum planning and course development.

And then there could be almost an infinite flexibility in the arrangements for the teachers and the taught, carefully organized to meet individual schedules, changes in interests and needs, and so on. The continuing education of an individual could be recorded as a story of individual growth and discovery, not just of credits.

Perhaps most important to Chamberlain is the possibility that

> ... the business world could be brought back into the cultural mainstream, as an integral part of our nation's intellectual activity. Is it too farfetched to imagine that our major corporations might begin appointing vice presidents in charge of education, not job training in the old sense, but genuine honest-to-goodness education, that youngsters entering the job market might select one company over another, or one community over another, because it offered them superior educational facilities? Is it too fanciful to conceive of job seekers pouring through corporate course catalogues with an interest at least equal to that which they might now give to a statement of wage policy, working conditions and fringe benefits?

Nor does he shy away from the possible need for public financing.

> To the extent that enlightened public economic policy continues to lessen the danger of recurring recessions, and continuing education proves effective in making our labor force more adaptable and upgradable, funds now allocated to the alleviation of unemployment or accelerated retirement may be at least partially diverted to educational financing. From whatever source the financing comes, it constitutes a genuine social investment, paying dividends in the form of a more productive work force. In a real sense, investment in edu-

cation is self-financing over a time, even though the degree to which this is true is largely unmeasurable.[4]

The prospect is an interesting one and it may well come to pass. What seems to be happening is a recognition that learning, living, and working cannot be separated and that the institutions that society organizes to meet these needs, public and private, will become increasingly inter-related and mixed. Our traditional educational agencies will continue to carry the main burden of preparing people for life and for careers, but already in a very real sense the factory and the office have also become schools, creating new problems of educational goals, articulation and definition of institutional responsibility.

Second careers for businessmen. The combination of longer life spans and earlier retirements raises the possibility of second careers for those businessmen for whom golf and fishing are not consuming passions. The "senior citizen" group has long been discussed as a social and economic problem; it is only slowly coming to be considered a potential reservoir of experience and knowledge. Many corporations are now encouraging early retirement of employees at fifty-five years of age and, in some cases, earlier. Union contracts have been negotiated which provide for earlier retirement or periodic long, thirteen-week vacations. This provides a pool of talent which might be used to provide service to the economy and help guarantee its growth. A number of retired executives have already volunteered to serve as management consultants to the governments of newly developing countries in Asia, Africa, and Latin America. Others are working as advisers to small businessmen or social agencies in their own communities. For many active individuals, such participation is far more rewarding than a passive submission to a life of aimless leisure to which they are neither accustomed nor inclined.

The present efforts of business firms to prepare their older employees for retirement are restricted to the dissemination of information on pensions, budgets, and the benefits of periodic physical examinations. It may be possible, however, for business—perhaps in cooperation with government—to assume a more direct responsibility for the re-education of these people for new careers and new positions of responsibility. If an economy is to expand, it must

---

[4] Neil W. Chamberlain, "The Corporation as a College," copyright © 1956 by The Atlantic Monthly Co., Boston, Mass., June 1965, p. 104.

exploit all available resources and remove the arbitrary limits set upon the usefulness of the most important of all resources: the human being.

Programs might be worked out between government and industry whereby employees planning to retire early might undergo partially subsidized training to enter such fields as teaching, social and church work, or community service. Such programs could be developed jointly by government agencies, universities, and business educators.

Aid to education. As America continues to grow in population, economic well-being, and international prestige, it will encounter more and more of the problems inherent in a rapidly changing society. The solution to many of these problems may well depend on the function of education. The vested interest of industry in a productive and harmonious society places its responsibilities to the schools in a new perspective.

It is difficult, if not impossible, to assess the contribution of the schools to our society. Eli Ginzberg of Columbia University points out that the public school system has helped to establish a set of common values, tastes, and attitudes—thus speeding the change from a group of loosely associated political entities to one, united nation. It is the general level of education provided by the schools which has provided the technological base and leadership potential essential to economic expansion.

Unfortunately, however, the schools too are faced with the problems engendered by a rapidly changing society. The same explosion of knowledge and information which has caused a re-evaluation of industrial procedures also carries consequences for the educational system. If the schools are to continue to contribute to the progress and well-being of the society, they must be able to provide the rising levels of technical and general education now demanded of all members of the labor force of the nation. This means that the schools must have the funds to obtain the materials for instruction, to attract intelligent and dedicated teachers, to build larger and more modern plants, and to provide the longer and more specialized education required. If the schools are to turn out well-educated, well-prepared, well-adjusted members of society, they must have the resources with which to meet their responsibilities and fulfill their function. Even more important, they must have the leadership that will encourage the effort to find new ways and means of adapting to the changes in the society as a whole.

There is slowly but constantly increasing support for the notion that some of the resources and leadership required by the schools might eventually come to be provided by business and industry. To those who argue that private enterprise must remain distinct—and, therefore, aloof—from the public section, one need only point out that the "private" decisions of the modern corporation affect not only its employees, stockholders, and customers, but larger so-society as well. Why then should not this influence be brought to bear on the problems of that society? Certainly the increasing complexities of life in the modern United States have created a demand for services which lie beyond the scope of private enterprise. This demand makes inevitable a reassessment of the respective roles of the public and private sectors in the American economy. The problem is to find the way by which these roles may be adapted to meet the demand, but without subverting the primary values upon which the society rests.

The presence of the corporation is being felt in a number of other areas as well. For example, a number of companies cooperate with community groups designed to bring about reforms and improvements in local public schools. The role of the corporation in public service activities may be seen in IBM's support of the National Education Association Project on the Educational Implications of Automation, the Esso Age of Kings program, and the RCA Science Seminar.

Conclusions

Industry's approach to its new public role has been a cautious one. There are many business leaders who insist that the activities described above do not lie within the proper scope of private enterprise. On the whole, however, the growth of the corporations has tended to bring about a realization of the new responsibilities imposed by size and influence. And there is also a new willingness to divert some of the enormous resources of American industry to the needs and welfare of the American society, as well as the development of the nations dealt with in their international operations.

A brief history and review of some of the major educational activities of business, as outlined in this book, should suggest to professional educators and administrators many opportunities for research and study. It should also suggest the possibility of developing new careers within business and industry in which educational training will be an important prerequisite. These two aspects should be of particular importance to those engaged in teacher and administrator training and curriculum development.

It is hoped also that the material presented will be of interest to the school administrators in public and higher education insofar as it outlines many activities within the business and industry scene which impinge upon their own work.

Since, in our opinion, the growth of educational activities within business and industry must inevitably grow, and probably at a rate faster than other functions, the building of better ties between educators in business and industry and their colleagues in professional education should be most fruitful.

Bibliography

Aid-to-Education Programs of Some Leading Business Concerns. New York: Council for Financial Aid to Education, Inc., 1964.

Bailyn, Bernard, *Education in the Forming of American Society.* New York: Vintage Books, 1960.

Bergevin, Paul, *Industrial Apprenticeship.* New York: McGraw-Hill Publishing Company, 1947.

Brown, J. Douglas, and Frederick Harbison, *High-Talent Manpower for Science and Industry.* Princeton: Industrial Relations Section, Princeton University, 1957.

Burns, Tom, and G. M. Stalker, *The Management of Innovation.* Chicago: Quadrangle Books, 1962.

Chamberlain, Neil W., "Job Obsolescence: Challenge and Opportunity," *The Educational Record,* January 1963, pp. 26–32.

Clark, H. F., and Sloan, H. S., *Classrooms in the Factories.* New York: New York University Press, 1958.

Cremin, Lawrence, *The Transformation of the School.* New York: Alfred A. Knopf, 1961.

Developing Better Managers: An Eight-Nation Study. Walter S. Wikstrom, ed., New York: National Industrial Conference Board, Inc., 1961.

Evans, Luther, and Arnstein, George, *Automation and the Challenge to Education.* Washington, D.C.: National Education Association, 1962.

Haire, Mason, "The Social Sciences and Management Practices," *California Management Review.* Summer 1964, pp. 3–10.

Harbison, Frederick, and Charles A. Myers, *Education, Manpower and Economic Growth.* New York: McGraw-Hill Book Company, 1964.

Human Progress through Better Management, Proceedings of the CIOS XIII, International Management Congress. New York: Council for International Progress in Management, 1963.

Lyons, E. H., and Wilson, James W., *Work-Study College Programs.* New York: Harper & Row Publishers, 1961.

Manpower Report of the President. Washington, D.C.: U.S. Government Printing Office, March 1963 and March 1964.

Mayo, Elton, *The Social Problems of an Industrial Civilization.* Cambridge: Harvard University Press, 1945.

Mee, John F., *Management Thought in a Dynamic Economy.* New York: New York University Press, 1963.

Merrill, Harwood F., ed., *Classics in Management.* New York: American Management Association, 1960.

Roethlisberger, F. J. and Dickson, W. J., *Management and the Worker.* Cambridge: Harvard University Press, 1939.

Schein, E., "Management Development As a Process of Influence," *Industrial Review.* Vol. 1, No. 1, May 1961.

Schultz, Theodore W., *The Economic Value of Education*. New York: Columbia University Press, 1963.

Serbein, Oscar N., *Educational Activities of Business*. Washington, D.C.: American Council on Education, 1961.

Siegle, Peter E., *New Directions in Liberal Education for Executives*. Chicago: The Center for the Study of Liberal Education for Adults, 1958.

Silk, Leonard S., *The Education of Businessmen*. New York: Committee for Economic Development, 1960.

Simon, Herbert, *The New Science of Management Decision*. New York: Harper & Row, 1960.

U.S. Chamber of Commerce—Washington Reports—Special Supplements, *Manpower Development and Training Kit (0577)*. Washington, D.C.: 1964.

U.S. Department of Labor, *Apprenticeship—Past and Present*. Washington, D.C.: U.S. Government Printing Office, 1962.

Venn, Grant, *Man, Education, and Work*. Washington, D.C.: American Council on Education, 1964.

Index